Dolphins
and Porpoises

Dolphins and Porpoises

Louise Quayle

Illustrations by Pieter A. Folkens

HEADLINE

A FRIEDMAN GROUP BOOK

Copyright © 1989 Michael Friedman Publishing Group, Inc.

First published in Great Britain in 1989
by HEADLINE BOOK PUBLISHING PLC

First published in softback
by HEADLINE BOOK PUBLISHING PLC

British Library Cataloguing in Publication Data

Quayle, Louise
 Dolphins and porpoises.
 1. Dolphins and porpoises
 I. Title
 599.5'3

ISBN 0-7472-7954-3

DOLPHINS AND PORPOISES
A Complete Photographic and Scientific Survey
was prepared and produced by
Michael Friedman Publishing Group, Inc.
15 West 26th Street
New York, New York 10010

Editor: Sharon Kalman
Art Director: Robert W. Kosturko
Designer: Devorah Levinrad
Illustrator: Pieter A. Folkens
Photography Editor: Christopher Bain
Photo Researcher: Daniella Nilva
Production Manager: Karen L. Greenberg

Typeset by Mar + X Myles Graphics, Inc.
Color Separations by South Sea International Press, Ltd.
Printed and bound in Hong Kong by Leefung-Asco Printers, Ltd.

The quote that appears on page 113 by Ken Norris is from The Porpoise Watcher,
courtesy of W.W. Norton & Company, Inc.

HEADLINE BOOK PUBLISHING PLC
Headline House
79 Great Titchfield Street
London W1P 7FN

DEDICATION

To my mother, whose commitment to recycling and ecology has been,
despite all my efforts to the contrary, an inspiration.

ACKNOWLEDGMENTS

I am grateful to the many people who, directly and indirectly, helped in the writing of this book.
Thanks to Joan Ward, at the Office of Public Information of the University of California, Santa Cruz,
who generously offered help in collecting research materials and photographs, to Stan Minasian
of the Marine Mammal Fund for his comments on dolphin/tuna fishing, and to Lawrence Barnes of the
Natural History Museum of Los Angeles County. Thanks also to the staff at the
Michael Friedman Publishing Group: to Karla Olson for her friendship and for taking a risk on an
untested writer; to Sharon Kalman and Devorah Levinrad for putting it all together;
and to Chris Bain for his diligent pursuit of the illustrative material.
Many thanks are due to Robin for introducing me to the Whale Center, and to Philippa for her patient ear.
Finally, I am indebted to Pieter Folkens of the Oceanic Society in San Francisco for reviewing the text.
He suffered through long hours on the telephone, even when the World Series, pesto, or Arend had to
wait. I am particularly grateful for his comments on evolution and intelligence, for his referrals to other
illustrative and research sources, and for pointing me to Joseph Campbell and modern myth-making.
Pieter also has a knack for unscrambling mixed metaphors. And, of course, without his
illustrations and photographs this book would be sorely lacking.

CONTENTS

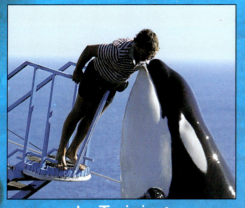

Chapter One
Of Gods and Dolphins

Dolphins and porpoises have intrigued humans for centuries. Whether viewed as playful friends, divine gods, or pesky nuisances, these whale relatives have been revered or despised in nearly all coastal cultures since the beginning of time. The Greek word *delphys*, meaning womb, the root of the word "dolphin," signifies the Greeks' reverence for their gods in dolphin form.

Dolphins have been worshipped by both Eastern and Western maritime coastal societies that shaped our own modern cultures, and by ancient goddess religions predating the Greeks.

While Greek gods celebrated the power of humans over their environment, the religions of the goddess worshipped our connection to earth and the life-giving power of the soil and sea of which we are a part. Today, many people turn to this early dolphin mythology to regain just one of the many ways in which our reverence for nature has been lost or gone awry.

Both the history of the scientific study of dolphins and the history of their religious and cultural symbolism reach back nearly to the beginning of civilization. As long ago as 2200 BC, dolphins appeared on cave walls in Norway. From the deserts of the Near and Middle East to Asia to Western Europe, dolphin images have been found on pottery, coins, and statues, and dolphin legend has been recorded in literature and song. From these archaeological, artistic, and religious discoveries to the story of a boy and his dolphin on prime-time TV, to today's efforts to save depleted and endangered species from ruthless fishing practices and harmful waste in the oceans, dolphins are inextricably woven into our consciousness.

T his Greek amphora, coins, and necklace were among the many treasured objects adorned with the powerful image of the dolphin, which signified safe travel and good luck.

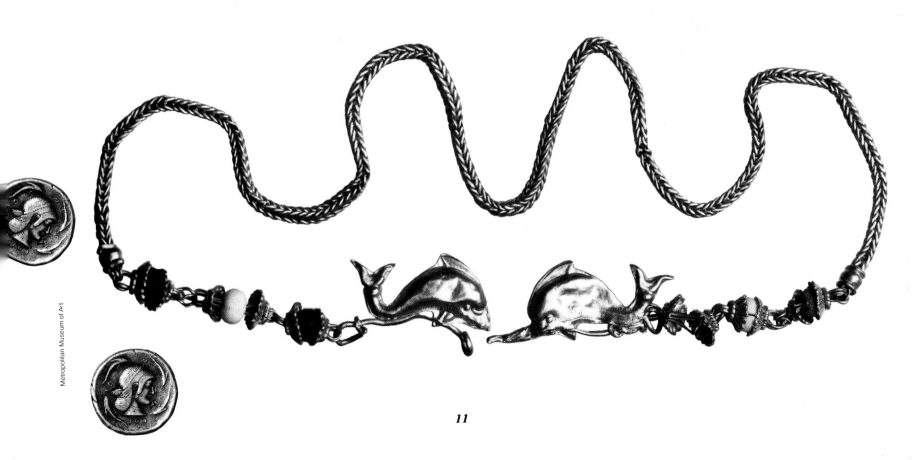

Metropolitan Museum of Art

North Wind Picture Archive

DOLPHIN MYTHOLOGY

As with many other mysteries of the natural world, the Greeks contributed a considerable amount to our knowledge of dolphins. Greek gods, who possessed human attributes as well as magical, mythical powers, sometimes took the form of dolphins. These marine mammals were interwoven with the lives of the gods and goddesses whose actions formed moral allegories for Greek life. Apollo, Demeter, and Aphrodite are among the deities with whom dolphins have been associated.

Greek curiosity about dolphins was manifest in their religious statuary and temples. The temple Delphi on Mt. Parnassus, a religious site for hundreds of years before the Greeks built the temple there between the sixth and seventh centuries BC, honored the oracle of the god Apollo. As early as the fourteenth century BC, worshippers could come to the oracle here—known then as Pytho—and divine the teachings of Gaia, Mother Earth. According to Greek myth, Apollo, the god of light, reason, and culture, battled with Python, the serpent daughter of Gaia, to establish his own oracle. Apollo then took the form of a herd of dolphins and led a lost ship from Crete to the Gulf of Corinth, about six miles from Mt. Parnassus. The sailors, awed with the role these powerful creatures had played in saving their lives, vowed to serve the oracle of Apollo and renamed it Delphi in honor of his dolphin form.

The oracle of Apollo was believed to be the center of the universe. The Greeks asked the oracle for guidance on personal matters as well as on decisions affecting their government. On the seventh day of the Delphic month, Apollo's birthday, the traditional medium called the Pythia, a woman over fifty dressed in maiden's clothing, would enter the temple and eat laurel leaves (Apollo's sacred tree); she then would speak the wisdom of the oracle.

©FPG International

I n one version of the myth that established Apollo's

oracle at Delphi (left), he rides the stormy seas of the Medi-

terranean on the back of a dolphin. The Treasure House at

Delphi (above), reconstructed with its original stone slabs, is

inscribed with musically notated hymns to Apollo.

*T*his dolphin fresco (below), at the Palace of Knossos

on the island of Crete is among some of the most famous

renderings of dolphins dating to ancient times. Right: To pre-

Hellenic cultures and to the Greeks, the temple at Delphi

was the center of the universe. Originally the temple of

Gaia—Mother Earth—Apollo overtook the oracle and

reigned supreme here for centuries. Today, many cite pre-

Hellenic art as evidence that the religions of the goddess

once ruled the earth in peace and harmony.

Many other pre-Hellenic cultures also worshipped dolphins. Friezes and frescoes of dolphins at the Aegean Palace of Knossos on the island of Crete are among the most well-known works of art of the ancient world. From the Minoans to the Mycenaeans and from the Phoenicians and Greeks to the Romans, dolphins appear in religious iconography as well as on everyday items such as vases, cups, and coins.

The Greek tradition was a strong influence on all subsequent cultures of the ancient and modern world. As the Greeks traded goods throughout the Mediterranean, their culture and religion spread, too. Dolphins were revered far inland as well as along the coast of the Mediterranean. To many early cultures, the dolphin was associated with safe travel, fertility, and their own destiny. The dolphin appeared in the myth and art of civilizations from the Orient to India, and from the Middle East to Europe. The Nabataean civilization, which spread inland from the Negev Desert to the land between the Tigris and Euphrates Rivers during their peak from the second century BC to the second century AD, drew much of their religious symbolism from Hellenistic examples. Like the Greek gods, Nabataean deities often took the form

of, or were depicted with, dolphins. The Nabataean goddess Atargatis took many forms, including the Fish Goddess, Dolphin Goddess, and Grain Goddess. Worshipped for safe travel on land and at sea, the Dolphin Goddess represented the harbinger of good weather, and was linked to the Nabataean concept of destiny. With coins bearing the images of dolphins in their hands, the dead were assured a safe journey to the afterlife.

As Nelson Glueck points out in his book *Deities and Dolphins,* the dolphin represented "succor in peril, safety in danger, security and promise of blessing in the unknown and hereafter." The goddess Atargatis represented the earth, the sea, and the sustenance of life. While one aspect of Atargatis, as the Fish Goddess, was associated with fertility, some scholars believe that the

separate attributes of the Fish and Dolphin goddesses blurred over time; or perhaps the Dolphin Goddess was one and the same with the Fish Goddess. As the Fish Goddess, Atargatis was "the female incarnate, whose bountiful womb made her the progenitress supreme. As the [Dolphin Goddess], she was a gracious sprite who calmed the seas and cleared the skies and conducted the traveler to safe havens during the limited span of mortality and through the endless reaches of afterlife."

Another Nabataean goddess depicted with dolphins was Galenaia, derived from the Greek Aphrodite, the goddess of sensual love, who was born from the foam of the sea. Galenaia represented good weather to the Nabataeans, on which their trading economy depended. One of the four sacred elements of life,

water is a giver and sustainer of life, and dolphins were intimately connected with that symbolism.

The Nabataean society is but one example of a culture that revered dolphins. Dolphins also appear in Roman statuary, most notably that of Eros riding a dolphin at Aphrodite's side, and on a Jewish sarcophagus dating to the second century AD at Beit She'arim, near Haifa. The fish/dolphin symbol was significant to Christians, too. For early Christians, the dolphin was a symbol of rebirth, of "the intercessor who guided and supported man in the sea and allowed him to return to land cleansed of his sins." It is believed that even the secret symbol of the fish, which marked the meeting place for persecuted Christians, may actually have derived from dolphin symbology.

On this sarcophagus displayed at the Musée du Louvre, in Paris, France, dolphins romp playfully with nymphs, long-lived Greek mythological figures. In some cultures, dolphins ensured a safe journey to the afterlife.

North Wind Picture Archives

UNDERSTANDING LIFE AT SEA

Religion is sometimes seen as a reflection of humans' attempt to understand nature, science as a way to control it. Even as their mythology revered dolphins, the Greeks also studied the realities of the dolphins' life at sea. In *History of Mammals,* Aristotle (384-322 BC) was the first to identify that dolphins and porpoises were separate animals and to accurately record the behavior of dolphins. Later, the Roman scholar Pliny (AD 23-79) wrote about dolphins in his book *Natural History,* basing many of his conclusions on fantastical tall tales from fishermen. His is the first written account of the relationship between fishermen and dolphins, noting that fishing boats often followed dolphins in pursuit of their catch. Like the Greeks, the people of Pliny's time had tre-

mendous respect for dolphins, but instead of attributing godlike powers to them Pliny embellished stories of their songs and friendliness, making them nearly human. Dolphins do sing, and stories of their affection for each other and for humans are based in fact, yet Pliny tended to exaggerate the meaning of their behavior. As more became known about dolphins' sophisticated abilities, their significance as mythical creatures grew.

Dolphins' "friendliness" continued to captivate the human imagination. In *Aesop's Fables,* the dolphin appeared as the voice of reason. Yet as the centuries passed and religious philosophers and scientists began to view "man" as the center of the universe, the dolphin began to be seen more and more in human

Aristotle (opposite page) was the first to record the behavior of dolphins and porpoises and to identify them as distinct members of the same mammalian order. His book History of Mammals *was a source for later Roman scholars such as Pliny.*

Modeled on a fresco by the Italian Renaissance artist Raphael, this engraving (left) shows two dolphins towing the figure of the Greek sea nymph Galatea.

©Howard Hall

Above: *Spotted dolphins.* Opposite page: *Film-makers record the activities of killer whales in their own habitat in Johnstone Strait, British Columbia.*

terms. The thirteenth-century *Gesta Romanorum* tells the story of a boy and dolphin who become devoted to each other. One day the dolphin does not appear and the boy drowns as the tide comes in while he sits and waits for the animal's return. When the tide recedes, the dolphin comes back to find the boy dead, and, in turn, dies of grief.

While the stories in *Gesta Romanorum* were intended as moralistic parables, the idea that dolphins were capable of emotion and, thus, possessed a brain complex enough to make them truly sentient beings has created controversy in the scientific community. During the sixteenth century, scientists began to make the connection between the human brain and its role in controlling the body and the idea of "mind." As John Lilly, a theorist on dolphin communication, observed, "At the times of the Greeks and Romans there was little, if any, link made between brain and mind. Scholars attributed man's special achievements to other factors than excellence of brain structure and its use." Out of these discoveries grew the study of brain size in relation to a creature's intelligence. By 1843, noting that the dolphin brain was large in proportion to its body size, Sir William Jardine ventured in *The Naturalist's Library* that the dolphin was "of more than ordinary wit and capacity."

As science began to compare dolphins to humans, the animals' mythological significance changed, too. With knowledge of their superior intelligence, the power of dolphins now had solid scientific backing. As our knowledge of their intelligence and ability to communicate grew, so did our proclivity to accord them powers unknown in other animals. John Lilly believed that dolphins would one day be able to talk with us, bringing their superior intellect to bear on the human condition.

Today, knowledge of dolphin intelligence and communication has inspired a new generation of mythmakers that places dolphins among the gods. Followers of the Gaia Hypothesis, which says that the earth and everything on it or in it is woven into one giant living system, would say that the exploitation of dolphins by tuna fishing and the destruction of their environment by pollutants harms humans directly. According to the Gaian, the well-being of all living things on earth is sacred while humans have "set [themselves] over and above the material world, to think of nature as merely the backdrop to the human drama." Only by returning to a healthy relationship with and reverence for nature, of which we are a part, can we expect our planet to survive. More than an active awareness of ecology and the environment, Gaian consciousness strives to incorporate humans' lost sense of the divine in nature. Perhaps dolphins can once again become symbols of that quest.

©Frank S. Balthis

Joseph Campbell, the author of *The Hero with a Thousand Faces,* wrote that humans have lost those traditional myths that link them to nature and to their culture. Campbell believed that we need to create new myths to shape us once again into a holistic society in which we feel a connection with nature as well as with our culture. With such a mythological and spiritual understanding, humans would be equipped to live peacefully and in harmony with earth, rather than as beings at the center of the universe who controlled it. The technology and science of our modern world has split us from nature and earth, yet Campbell argues that rather than reject science—rather than use it as a tool of reckless destruction—we can use it to inform our sense of wonder.

A world that values the material over the natural and places humans at the center of the universe can only view dolphins' extraordinary qualities as tools to control and exploit. Today, as more and more people realize that human "control" of the environment has placed us in great danger, a few take steps to a time before the Greeks when integrating and maintaining Mother Earth meant as much to us as our contemporary drive to maintain a quality of life at the expense of our children and our planet. On the prime-time TV show "Flipper," the dolphin often led his friend Sandy to new fishing grounds; through understanding the aquatic life of dolphins and porpoises perhaps we can begin to offer the real Flippers—and ourselves—more hospitable rivers and oceans.

Chapter Two
Origins of the Odontocetes

ike humans, dolphins and porpoises are warm-blooded, air-breathing mammals that evolved from a parallel, though unrelated, group of ancestors to those of humans. Their ability to utilize echolocation, a form of sonar, and the ease with which some dolphins are trained has generated a modern mythical version of this special animal. We tend to forget that, like all

other animals, they evolved to fill a particular niche in the world's ecosystem.

Still, the link between marine and terrestrial mammals has puzzled scientists for centuries. All mammals evolved from warm-blooded, mammal-like reptiles about 190 million years ago. When the dinosaurs disappeared about sixty-five million years ago, major environmental niches opened which were filled by the rapid adaptation of early mammals. Millions of years of evolution among mammals on land and in the sea divided the mammals into the condylarths and insectivores, and carnivores (flesh-eaters). Cetaceans (whales and dolphins) evolved out of the ungulates. The cetacean bone structure is similar to other mammals (whales' and dolphins' flippers resemble general mammalian digitation), and comparisons of the fetal blood sugars of whales and dolphins with those of the even-toed ungulates like deer and cattle support the theory that they have a common ancestor.

B*elow: Researchers get a close look at spotted dolphins in the Bahamas. Members of the subfamily Delphininae, the most modern branch of the family Delphinidae, evolved about ten million years ago from the ancient dolphins. Note their sharply demarcated snouts and falcate dorsal fins.* Right: *Three members of the Delphininae family break the surface.*

©Marty Snyderman

©Carl Roessler/FPG International

THE DOLPHIN AND PORPOISE FAMILIES

All dolphins and porpoises are members of the Cetacea. Dolphins and porpoises belong to Ondontoceti, one of the two living suborders of the Cetacea. Members of the Cetacea evolved their own special physical and behavioral characteristics to survive in their aquatic environment. Dolphins and porpoises adapted echolocation, developing a single prey-item feeding strategy: in other words, they hunt and eat fish one at a time. Another fundamental characteristic that identifies dolphins and porpoises as odontocetes is their teeth (in fact, "odontocete" means "toothed whale"). Their relatives the Mysticeti, the suborder made up of what most think of as whales, are identified by their baleen plates, with which they feed on tiny, shrimplike krill and other zooplankton. Most scientists have accepted that both the Mysticeti and Odontoceti evolved from the same ancestor. Nevertheless, dolphins and porpoises possess many specializations that place them in distinct families within the suborder Odontoceti.

Among the ten living families of Odontoceti, six contain dolphins and porpoises. The Delphinidae (oceanic dolphins, split into two subfamilies Delphininae [dolphins] and Globicephalinae [pilot whales]), Phocoenidae (porpoises), and Platanistidae (river dolphins, split into four subfamilies, Pontoporidae, Inidae, Lipotidae, and Platanistae) are described throughout this book. Other families of the Odontoceti include Physeteridae (sperm whales), Monodontidae (narwhal and beluga whales), and Ziphiidae (beaked whales), all of which are the toothed relatives of dolphins and porpoises.

Odontocetes evolved a skull and rostrum that over millions of years has telescoped gradually. The melon at the top of the rostrum, in front of the forehead; the nasal diverticula, the vestibular sacs that open from the blowhole; and, in the sperm whale, the spermaceti organ are all specializations that distinguish them from the mysticetes. Dolphins and porpoises also emit higher frequency sounds than other cetaceans, which they use in echolocation to hunt as well as to communicate. And unlike their mysticete relatives, most odontocetes, particularly killer whales and oceanic dolphins, are highly socialized, traveling in large herds. Beaked whales and river dolphins are more solitary members of the suborder, usually traveling alone.

The evolution of dolphins can be traced through the gradual telescoping of their skulls and rostrum. On the mesonychid skull (between sixty-five and forty million years old) the nares appear at the tip of the snout. As the order Archaeocete evolved, the nares moved up the snout as its tip lengthened. Note that the front of the snout of Basilosaurus (forty-eight to thirty-six million years ago) is longer than that of its predecessor Remingtonocetus (fifty to forty-six million years ago). As we approach the modern dolphin, the prehistoric odontocete Squalodont (twenty-eight to eleven million years ago) has the long snout similar to the modern Lipotes vexillifer (Beiji). Its nares are slightly forward on its head and four of its teeth protrude beyond the tip of its snout.

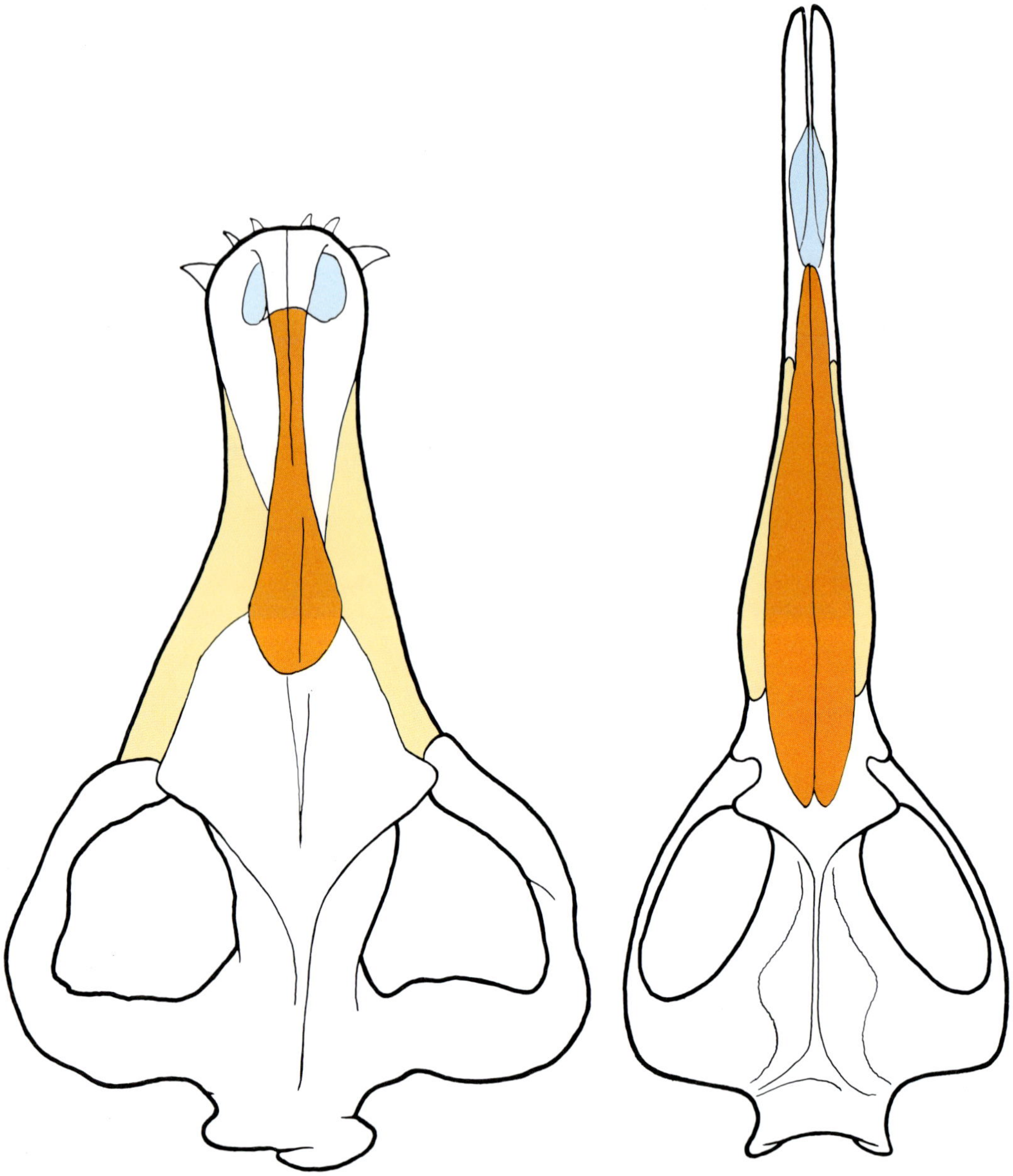

☐ NARIAL PASSAGE, NARES (BLOWHOLE)

■ NASAL BONES

■ MAXILLA BONES

Mesonychid
Pre-Cetacean

Remingtonocetus harudiensis
Early Archaeocete

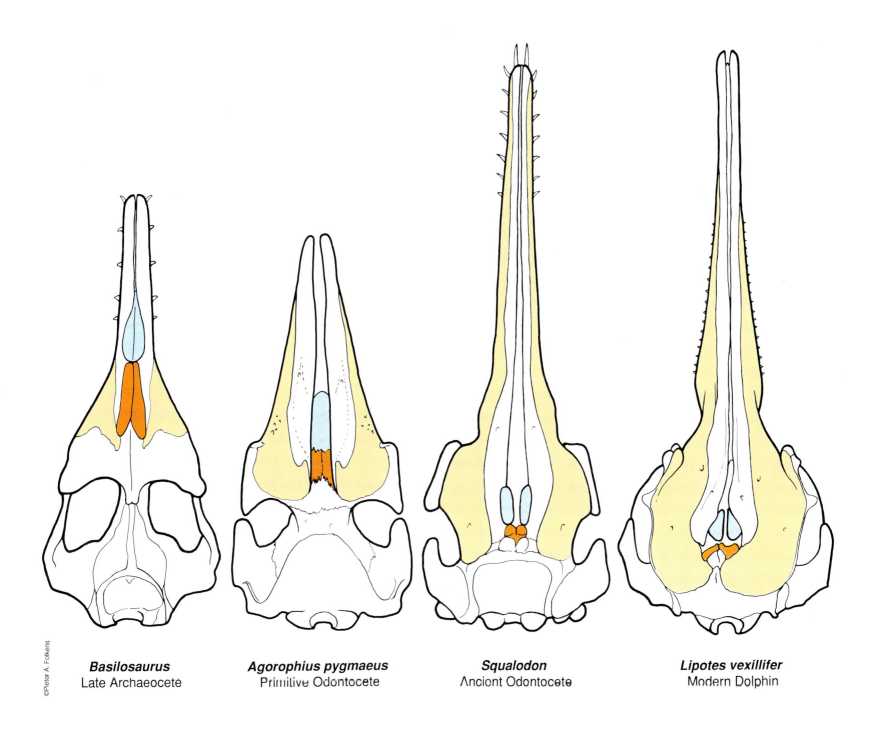

©Pieter A. Folkens

Basilosaurus
Late Archaeocete

Agorophius pygmaeus
Primitive Odontocete

Squalodon
Ancient Odontocete

Lipotes vexillifer
Modern Dolphin

©Frank S. Balthis

Above: *The Long Marine Lab at the University of California at Santa Cruz is home to one of the country's foremost dolphin research centers. Here, the skull and bones of a dolphin are assembled.* Right: *At Sharktooth Hill, California, paleontologists uncovered this ancient dolphin rostrum and skull. Note the long snout on the skull.*

©Pieter A. Folkens

The chart on the following page illustrates the members of the three dolphin and porpoise families. The family Delphinidae consists of the Oceanic Dolphins (including the killer whale, the common and bottlenose dolphins, and the spotted dolphins). The family Phocoenidae, the True Porpoises, includes the harbor porpoise, the Cochito, and the finless porpoise. The family Plantanistidae contains the River Dolphins and the Franciscana.

THE FAMILY TREE

Like clues in a treasure hunt, the fossil remains of whale and dolphin ancestors provide only a tantalizing glimpse of what we know of the three suborders of the Cetacea—the Mysticeti, Odontoceti, and the extinct Archaeoceti. Sometimes only fragments—a skull or teeth or a portion of bone—are found to identify a particular family. Years of analysis and research are required to properly identify each find, and then a more recent discovery may throw the present taxonomy into question. To frustrate matters, lack of research funds leaves many finds sitting in warehouses waiting for analysis.

The fossil record for cetaceans is far from complete. Some prehistoric whales lived where fossilized remains have yet to surface. Buried in sediment in the ocean floor, it could take millions of years before these fossilized remains reach the surface. Sedimentary rock that we can reach which contains whale fossils is found in only a few places in the eastern United States, California, Mexico, northern Italy, West Germany, India, Pakistan, and New Zealand. Dating the fossils is based only on the known layers found at the surface; millions of years of evolution is sometimes left to sophisticated guesswork. While some scientists are challenging existing evolutionary theory with cytogenetics—a method by which the molecular structure of living species is compared to fossils—it must be tested before venturing any conclusions.

PYGMY KILLER WHALE

MELON-HEADED WHALE

BOUTU

FRANCISCANA

INDUS SUSU

GANGES SUSU

BEIJI

KILLER WHALE

FALSE KILLER WHALE

SHORT-FINNED PILOT WHALE

HECTOR'S DOLPHIN

HEAVISIDE'S DOLPHIN

BLACK DOLPHIN

COMMERSON'S DOLPHIN

LONG-FINNED PILOT WHALE

IRRAWADDY DOLPHIN

©Pieter A. Folkens

PEALE'S DOLPHIN

ATLANTIC HUMP-BACKED DOLPHIN

COMMON DOLPHIN

PACIFIC WHITE-SIDED DOLPHIN

INDO-PACIFIC HUMP-BACKED DOLPHIN

STRIPED DOLPHIN

ATLANTIC WHITE-SIDED DOLPHIN

BOTTLENOSE DOLPHIN

CLYMENE DOLPHIN

SPINNER DOLPHIN

WHITE-BEAKED DOLPHIN

PANTROPICAL SPOTTED DOLPHIN

SPOTTED DOLPHIN

FRASER'S DOLPHIN

DUSKY DOLPHIN

NORTHERN RIGHT WHALE DOLPHIN

ROUGH-TOOTHED DOLPHIN

HOURGLASS DOLPHIN

SOUTHERN RIGHT WHALE DOLPHIN

BURMEISTER'S PORPOISE

HARBOR PORPOISE

TUCUXI

FINLESS PORPOISE

COCHITO PORPOISE

RISSO'S DOLPHIN

DALL'S PORPOISE

SPECTACLED PORPOISE

ARCHAEOCETE: THE ANCIENT WHALES

Scientists now believe that all whales and dolphins evolved from land-dwelling, wolflike creatures of the order *Condylarthra*, which lived more than fifty-eight million years ago during the Paleocene Era. Were we to see one today, it would not resemble the fully aquatic cetacean at all. Some condylarths of the family Mesonychidae evolved to exploit the niche vacated by the ichthyosaurs, carniverous aquatic dinosaurs, who died out fifteen million years earlier at the end of the Cretaceous period. These terrestrial mammals gave rise to the ancient whales, the archaeocetes, as well as to the Artidactyla, the modern ungulates, at the close of the Paleocene.

The family Mesonychidae, the ancestors of the even-toed ungulates as well as whales, lived along the edges of the Tethys Sea, and fed on shells and oysters. As the Mesonychid tail became flatter, its teeth sheared its catch, and its hooves disappeared. To make the full transition from land to water, descendents of the mesonychids, ancestral to the archaeocetes, developed a flatter tail, shorter limbs, and lost their hair, which would slow them down in the water. To provide insulation in their new marine environment, while the archaeocetes still had hind legs, their tails gradually became muscular and flatter evolving into one that would become a powerful locomotor in their new aquatic environment.

Millions of years ago the continents and seas as we know them looked very different. More than fifty-eight million years ago, most of the planet was covered with water. The edge of the ancient Tethys Sea, approximately where the Mediterranean and Persian Gulf are today, was home to the land-dwelling mesonychids. Over the next twenty million years, the continents expanded and the protocetaceans evolved specializations to sur-

vive in the harsh aquatic environment. These creatures were better adapted to surviving in the water. Archaeoceti hind legs were shorter than those of the mesonychids, while their bodies were slightly longer, making them more efficient swimmers. Their nostrils had inched up their skulls, which were becoming narrower. Two families of the Archaeocete, the Protocetidae and Basilosauridae, were closer to their predecessors than to modern whales, but their adaptations to marine life provide an important evolutionary link between today's dolphin and earth's earliest mammals.

Archaeoceti is divided into the families Protocetidae, Remingtonocetidae, and Basilosauridae (within which there are two subfamilies, Basilosaurinae and Dorudontinae). Our knowledge of their evolution has grown rapidly in little over 100 years. The fossilized remains of Basilosaurus, a member of the subfamily Basilosaurinae, were found as recently as 1832. While this creature was heralded as a typical archaeocete, its big, lumbering body is more analogous to a moray eel. Inhabiting marshy areas near shore in shallow water, basilosaurus would hide behind vegetation, snapping at its prey as it swam by. The discoverer thought it was a reptile, and originally dubbed the remains, which measured fifty feet (fifteen meters) long, "King Lizard." While basilosaurus remains tell us much about what the environment at the time was like, it is not a typical archaeocete.

Zygohriza, a member of the subfamily Durodontinae, more closely resembles the modern whale than all other archaeocetes. With a large body, a small head and beak, and flippers that could rotate in many directions to shimmy up to the shoreline, zygohriza was fully aquatic. Like the modern whale, zygohriza's blowhole was placed partway up the rostrum.

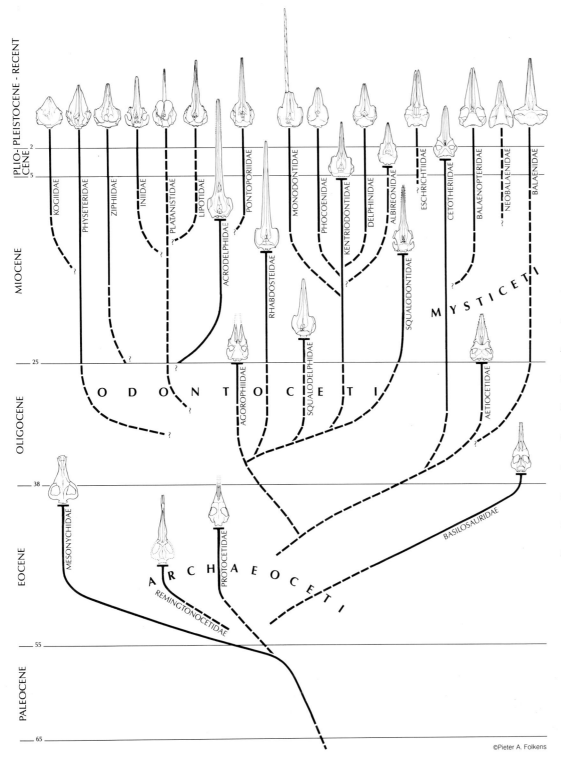

Thɪs phylogeny of cetacea shows the development of the shape of the skull for the various cetacean families. A new family, Remingtonocetidae, which appeared during the Eocene epoch, has been added to the ancient whale order Archaeocete; another new family, Albireonidae, has been added to the extinct odontocetes. Albireonidae is closely related to the Kentriodonts, from which modern dolphins and porpoises derive. When Kentriodontidae died out at the end of the Oligocene, several types of dolphinlike odontocetes continued to live into the mid-Miocene. The Kentriodontidae probably provided the ancestral roots for belugas, porpoises, and oceanic dolphins.

ZYGOHRIZA

SQUALODON

KENTRIODON

Z ygohriza (above), *an archaeocete, is one of the best*

examples of an ancient dolphinlike cetacean that shows

many of the characteristics of modern dolphins. This recon-

struction is based on a skeleton described by Remington

Kellogg in 1936. Note that the hind legs have not completely

disappeared. Squalodonts (middle) *appeared approximately*

ten million years after zygohriza disappeared (twenty-eight

million years ago). They have slightly longer snouts and a

more pronounced dorsal fin. Squalodonts probably share an

ancestor with Kentriodontidae (below), *which lived through*

the end of the Miocene and resembled modern dolphins.

MOVING TOWARD MODERNITY

At the close of the Eocene into the Oligocene, the face of the earth changed once again. Antarctica separated from South America, changing the circumpolar currents. The ocean became colder and the archaeocetes, unable to adapt to this change in climate, died out. During the late Oligocene a number of primitive odontocetes filled the niches left vacant by the demise of the archaeocetes. Among these, members of the Agorophiidae and Squalodontidae, two extinct families most closely related to modern dolphins and whales, are probably ancestral to modern odontocetes. While the Agorophiidae had sharp, conical teeth and medium-long beaks, their telescoped skulls more closely resembled modern whales.

The squalodons measured about three meters long. Their skulls were nearly fully telescoped, their nasal passages were further atop their heads and sloped backward, an adaptation that protected them from water entering their nostrils (see skull illustration, page 26). The squalodons' hind legs and pelvic structure was reduced and their necks were shortened but still highly movable. Scientists believe they had developed a dorsal fin and streamlined bodies ideal for swimming.

The squalodons shared a common ancestor with the family *Kentriodontidae* during the early Oligocene. These prehistoric mammals most closely resembled modern dolphins and possessed the preliminary adaptations for echolocation. The shape of their skulls suggests that they had developed the mechanisms for echolocation and that they used it.

As dolphin ancestors began to make the transition from land to sea about fifty-five million years ago, during the late Paleocene, they had to adapt from listening to air sounds to developing the ability to hear sounds under water, eventually emitting their own sounds. Under water, sound waves resonate, in effect creating a secondary sound source from the original. As the skull lengthened, the melon, nasal passages, and, in the sperm whale, the spermaceti organ evolved to hear, "see," and communicate in this new environment. An imaging system—echolocation—may have first appeared at this time.

Today's dolphin and porpoise families appeared during the late Miocene, between ten and fifteen million years ago. The modern families Delphinidae (oceanic dolphins), Phocoenidae (porpoises), and Monodontidae (beluga, or white, whales) all derived early in the Miocene from early kentriodonts.

A highly unusual modern family, the Platanistidae (river dolphins), also evolved in the Miocene period but fossils are scarce. While river dolphins' ancestors have been traced to the Oligocene, scientists aren't sure exactly how they derived. Their predecessors are believed to have had long snouts resembling the squalodonts, but paleontologists have yet to identify which one exactly. The Pontoporidae (estuarine dolphins) developed at this time, too, and are the only living odontocetes with symmetrical skulls.

Other families of the Odontoceti suborder, the Ziphiidae (beaked whales) and Physeteridae (sperm whales) date from middle Miocene and early Micocene periods. Here, too, their affinity to early odontocetes is unclear.

Perhaps we will never find the clue that will tell us exactly how dolphins and porpoises evolved from land-dwelling animals to air-breathing sea creatures. Our fascination with their story is heightened by the frustrations of piecing together the clues nature has sporadically left us. Adding to the frustration, the fossils that are found often sit unstudied. Scientists from the Los Angeles County Museum, for example, collected a vast number of late-middle Miocene fossils in the San Joaquin Valley in California. That collection, the largest and most diverse of its kind, now lays dormant in a warehouse, its mysteries unrevealed due to lack of research funds.

Even so, we have garnered a tremendous amount of knowledge about the ancient history of dolphins and porpoises in the last few years. If the pace of our discoveries is allowed to continue, we may gain even more insight in the next few decades. Knowing something of the treasures of their history, their living and breathing forms offer us an even more dynamic picture of their lives on earth.

©Ken Balcomb/EarthViews

©Marc Webber

*W*hite whales, (opposite page) *or belugas, are among the most common members of cetacea in captivity. Like their cousins in the family Delphinidae, these members of the family Monodontidae date to the early Miocene.*

*L*eft: *One of the Dusky dolphin's distinguishing characteristics is the curve of its flippers. These members of the* Lagenorhynchus *genus leap often, sometimes as many as forty to fifty times in a row.*

Chapter Three
Dolphin Biology: Aquatic Adaptations

Dolphins (Delphinidae, Pontoporidae, and Platanistidae) and porpoises (Phocoenidae) possess many similarities and differences at the same time. The differences, for example, between fresh- and saltwater families of dolphins can be quite pronounced, the river dolphins exhibiting the primitive characteristic of being able to move their heads from side to side.

Yet these animals are classified in the same suborder because they all have teeth. As we've seen, all animals must adapt to survive in their environments. Perhaps dolphins and porpoises particularly fascinate us because of the unique adaptation of echolocation with which they hunt and communicate. Humans often attempt to understand the world in their own terms, to anthropomorphize creatures who exhibit characteristics we believe to be uniquely our own. How is it then that these mammals can survive an aquatic habitat that is so hostile to our own survival? Our fundamental survival requirements are food, air, water, and shelter. The needs of dolphins and porpoises aren't so different, though their bodies have adapted to foraging for food in the water.

T*he two groups on this page exemplify countershading* (above,) *and no pattern at all* (below). *Dark coloring on the back of the animal and light coloring on its belly provides optimum camouflage for the harbor porpoise, tucuxi, rough-toothed dolphin, and bottlenose dolphin. Looking at these animals from below, they blend in against the surface of the water; from above, they blend in with the depth. Because of the low-visibility of the murky rivers and lagoons, the Beiji, Susu, Boutu, and the finless porpoise have no pattern at all, as they have no reason to hide.*

ROUGH-TOOTHED DOLPHIN

BOTTLENOSE DOLPHIN

HARBOR PORPOISE

TUCUXI

FINLESS PORPOISE

BEIJI

BOUTU (AMAZON RIVER DOLPHIN)

SUSU (GANGES RIVER DOLPHIN)

40

SOUTHERN RIGHT WHALE DOLPHIN

ORCA

DALL'S PORPOISE

HOURGLASS DOLPHIN

COMMERSON'S DOLPHIN

PACIFIC WHITE-SIDED DOLPHIN

COMMON DOLPHIN

PANTROPICAL SPOTTED DOLPHIN

STRIPED DOLPHIN

The killer whale, Dall's porpoise, the hourglass dolphin, and Commerson's dolphin exhibit high contrast disruptive color patterning (above). Their stark black-and-white coloration facilitates their hunting strategy: several individuals swimming in a group look like a school of smaller fish in the water where their visibility is severely limited. Stripes, bands, and spots are other variations of disruptive color patterning (below). The Pacific white-sided dolphin, common dolphin, and spotted and striped dolphin are difficult to see and can more easily sneak up on their prey or hide from a predator.

THERMOREGULATION, RESPIRATION, AND CIRCULATION

As air-breathing mammals, many of us probably wonder how marine mammals can survive their watery environment. Imagine what it would be like if we had to hold our breath for an extended period of time while chasing our prey. Our gangly arms and legs would create drag in the water, the fat that keeps us warm on land would not do so in water, our lung capacity would hinder us from long dives, and the location of our nostrils would make breathing difficult once we did surface. The cetacean's streamlined head, neck, and body and specialized respiratory system adequately compensated for these problems.

Thermoregulation, the ability of an animal to maintain its body temperature, is based on the ability of dolphins and porpoises to move blood to primary organs, the presence of blubber, and the ability to move the blood out to the flippers, just as humans maintain their body temperature with the aid of clothes. In dolphins and porpoises, the blubber varies in thickness between species according to their need for insulation and their metabolic rate. Additional fat in other organs such as the liver and muscle tissue and a special oil in the bones, as well as thin capillaries, helps the blubber draw warmth from blood flowing toward the body core and transfer it to the cooler blood flowing away from the heart. The blubber protects the vital blood-carrying capillaries from losing heat, as does the absence of many appendages like fingers and toes.

As with all mammals, the cetacean's ability to keep the blood warm and flowing within its body is related to its respiration rate and circulation. (Dolphins and porpoises breathe through a blowhole located at the top of their heads. The animals can open and close these crescent-shaped slits with a kind of muscular plug, allowing them to keep water out of their lungs when diving.) Cetaceans' blood makeup and special adaptations of their circulation allow them to breathe at a lower rate than land-dwelling mammals. In humans, the blood protein called hemoglobin carries oxygen throughout the body. As anyone who has tried to hold their breath for a long time knows, hemoglobin is not capable of conserving the oxygen in our blood for a very long time. While human blood also contains myoglobin, in whales, dolphins, and porpoises the myoglobin stores oxygen to be used by the animal to maintain its internal body temperature and provide oxygen to the brain while swimming or diving. It is this blood protein, in conjunction with the cetaceans' breathing patterns, that allow some species to remain submerged for as long as an hour. Dolphins and porpoises breathe rapidly at the surface, exchanging 90 percent of their air, while humans exchange only 5 to 15 percent in a breath. This rapid exchange charges the cetacean's blood with oxygen.

Heart rate and circulation are closely linked to an animal's respiration and its ability to keep warm. Scientists believe that when cetaceans dive their heart rates decrease, conserving the oxygen stored in the blood to be supplied to the brain, and keeping the animal's interior body temperature constant. Their circulation actually adjusts to accommodate the various depths of the water. To resupply the oxygen in its blood when it surfaces, its heart rate increases dramatically, rushing the needed supplies of oxygen through the lungs and blood to be stored for the next underwater stint.

Adapting to life underwater requires more than the simple ability to maintain warmth and carry a high supply of oxygen in the blood. Even if humans did possess myoglobin and blubber and had the ability to reduce their heart rates to conserve energy, their rigid rib cage and their inability to withstand carbon dioxide in the bloodstream and muscles would hinder them from extended periods underwater. The rib cage in cetaceans is strong enough and flexible enough to withstand the pressure at great depths. Cetaceans also do not suffer from nitrogen narcosis—or the bends—as humans do. When divers breathe oxygen underwater, nitrogen gas is released in the blood; if the diver surfaces too rapidly, the nitrogen expands, causing pain.

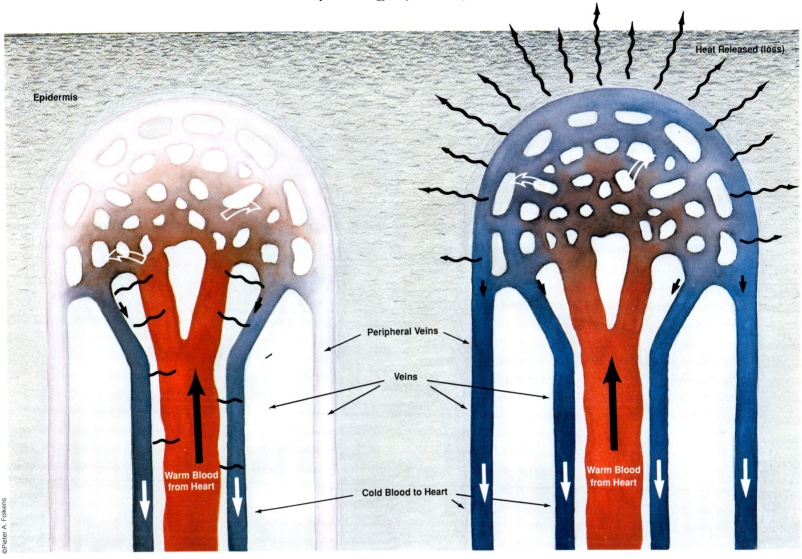

Epidermis

Heat Released (loss)

Peripheral Veins

Veins

Warm Blood
from Heart

Cold Blood to Heart

Warm Blood
from Heart

HEAT RETENTION

HEAT RELEASE

©Pieter A. Folkens

Divided into three layers—epidermis, dermis, and hypodermis for blubber—dolphin skin plays a vital role in maintaining body heat. These cross-sections show how the dolphin's circulation and its layers of skin regulate its body temperature. To cool off, the capillaries expand, allowing heat to be released through the epidermis. To keep warm, the artery contracts, keeping warm blood closer to the dolphin's body core.

LOCOMOTION

Whales, dolphins, and porpoises all have streamlined bodies, making them efficient swimmers. Their elongated heads blend with their bodies, and organs such as the ears and genitals—which are external in land mammals—are tucked away inside the body. Their ears, too, are little holes in the sides of their head which are filled with wax. Their muscular tails and flukes move in an up-and-down motion that drives them forward. The fatty and fibrous dorsal fin found on many species helps maintain their balance, though many whales and dolphins have little dorsal fin, if any. For them, the flippers play an even more important role in keeping them stable as well as in steering. Given that most dolphins feed on fish, squid, and, in the case of killer whales, other marine mammals, these animals have to move efficiently in the water to stalk their prey.

Below: Stenella longirostris, *the long-snouted spinner dolphin, leaps frequently as it swims. As with many other dolphins, the spinner dolphin's leaps help it to reserve energy. A dusky dolphin* (opposite page) *presents a spectacular view of its open blowhole, or nare, as it surfaces for a breath of air.*

©Marc Webber

To reduce the limitations of their heavy layer of blubber, it is attached not to the muscle but to an underlying system of ridges, which makes the blubber less resistant to drag. To further reduce drag in the water, their skin secretes oils (high polymer and ethyl oxide), which some scientists believe helps them shed skin cells. Just as an airplane is streamlined according to the principles of aerodynamics, the cetaceans efficiently move through the water according to theories known as "hydrodynamics" and "laminar flow." According to these scientific theories, the water closest to the skin creates the most drag, the production of oils lubricates the skin and helps the outer layers of water around the animal flow smoothly over each other.

Most dolphins are efficient swimmers. As cetacean expert David Gaskin explains, however, some species move more effi-ciently than others. The relation between the body thickness (and where the thickness is) and the degree to which the body is streamlined and tapered is known as the "fineness ratio." Small species of Delphinidae, for example, are the most streamlined. Some dolphins can move at twenty-one knots (thirty-nine kilometers per hour) in short spurts and maintain a normal speed of five to nine knots (nine to seventeen kilometers per hour). (See Chapter Four for specific information on individual species.)

One aspect of the way dolphins and porpoises swim which researchers have yet to fully explain are their frequent leaps into the air. While oceanarium shows in which dolphins perform may make you feel as though these moves are simply playful acrobatics, they may actually help the animal conserve energy and at the same time catch a breath of fresh air.

FEEDING AND DIGESTION

How well a dolphin moves in the water seems to be directly related to its feeding habits. One study of harbor porpoises showed that they spent only 3 percent of their time lying at the surface and about 21 percent of their time moving from one location to another. The rest of their time was spent looking for food. With that much energy used up with the simple process of moving, dolphins and porpoises can't afford to waste much energy savoring their meals. Most species have adapted mouth, tooth, and jaw structures that allow them to quickly puncture or tear at their prey and swallow them immediately. Dolphins and porpoises do not chew; their throats and stomachs can generally accommodate large chunks of food. In the human digestive system, saliva helps break down food for digestion in the stomach; because of their watery environment, dolphins have no saliva—the seawater would dilute it. Instead, all digestion takes place in their dual stomachs (see page 48).

The odontocetes can loosely be divided into three types of eaters: the fish eaters, squid eaters, and flesh eaters. The two groups of fish eaters—the Delphinidae and Phocoenidae—have slightly different adaptations to satisfy their mutual taste for herring, mackerel, cod, redfish, and, sometimes, squid. The Delphinidae generally have many sharp, pointy teeth housed in their slender rostrums. The Phocoenidae have chisel-shaped, "spatulate" teeth at a sharp angle to their jawlines, making them good at puncturing their food. The squid eaters—the Ziphiidae, pilot whales, and sperm whales—all exhibit variations in the number of teeth. Sperm whales, for example, have fewer upper teeth than the fish eaters, while pilot whales' teeth are mostly at the front of the mouth rather than running from the front to the back of the jaw. Ziphiidae family members may have few or no teeth at all. Killer whales and false killer whales, the only members in the flesh-eating category, have many sharp teeth in their upper and lower jaws, which they use to tear at the flesh of other marine mammals.

The coloring and markings of dolphins and porpoises also play a role in their feeding strategy. The pigmentation of dolphins

Slapping the water with their bodies (opposite page), killer whales will frighten their prey toward the shore. Sophisticated hunters, killer whales make full use of their large bodies to intimidate their prey.

With its rows of small, conical teeth, the bottlenose dolphin (right) punctures its food and swallows it whole or in large chunks without chewing.

and porpoises often serves as a kind of camouflage in the water.

The odontocete stomach is particularly well adapted to its feeding habits. Most dolphins and porpoises are opportunistic feeders, meaning they eat whenever the table is set, whether they're truly hungry or not. Compartmentalized into three sections, cetaceans' stomachs have more surface area and each compartment has its own job in the process of digestion—a sort of division of labor—which allows dolphins and porpoises to take full advantage of the nutrients they catch. The esophagus readily adapts to accommodate big chunks of food, sending it to the forestomach, where digestion begins; then the food passes to the second compartment, where the food is broken down into nutrients the animal can absorb; when the food finally passes to the third part of the stomach, any remaining nutrients pass into the blood stream. As with other mammals, the material that cannot be absorbed and used as nutirients passes through the intestines and out through the rectum.

SURVIVING

The basic facts of survival—keeping warm, moving efficiently in the water, and being able to eat—are similar in all species of dolphins and porpoises. Yet each species also has adapted specializations that scientists reevaluate constantly. Sleep, so important to humans, is something dolphins and porpoises engage in with only half their brains. Some, called the "surface sleepers," sleep suspended just below the surface, while others, the "bottom sleepers"—the river dolphins—sleep on the riverbed. However, neither the surface sleepers nor the bottom sleepers seem to need much sleep at all. While we utilize muscles all day to remain upright and maintain our balance, the force of gravity working on our bodies, dolphins are able to float, resting their muscles even if they're not sleeping. Additionally, unlike humans, who can take a breath of air at any time, dolphins must think to breathe. When they sleep, they use one half of their bicameral brain to rest, the other to maintain the all-important process of respiration.

While all dolphins and porpoises have some similar characteristics, others, like the sleeping behavior of oceanic and river dolphins, point to the subtle (and not so subtle) differences between the species. Even within the families of dolphins and porpoises, adaptation and speciation has led to their many distinct habits. All the members of the family are related, but each has its own special birthmark.

©Pieter A. Folkers

©Pieter A. Folkens

W*hile equipped with the same basic equipment for respiration, Dall's porpoise* (left)*, and the common dolphin* (above) *utilize different strategies for breathing. Dall's porpoise is sometimes called the "spray porpoise" for the vortex of air it creates around its blowhole to breathe. The animal conserves energy by not having to break the surface (see also page 76). The common dolphin jumps out of the water and breathes in the air.*

Chapter Four
Families in the Clan

While "dolphin" and "porpoise" are often used interchangeably to name air-breathing sea mammals, they are actually entirely different species belonging to distinct families within the toothed-whale (Odontoceti) suborder of the Cetacea. There are as many differences between the two families of dolphins—the river dolphins (Family Platanistidae) and the oceanic dolphins

(Family Delphinidae)—as there are between penguins and terns. Porpoises (Family Phocoenidae) are as distinct from dolphins as puffins are from gulls. As mammals, of course, dolphins and porpoises all breathe air and bear live young. As members of the Odontoceti suborder, all species possess teeth; a telescoped skull shape (though in some it is more pronounced than in others); the same up-and-down movement of their tails for swimming; a single nare (blowhole) at the top of the head for breathing; some ability to emit sound either to navigate, locate their prey, or communicate with each other; poor eyesight; and ears that are mere plugged-up holes at the side of the head. Dolphins and porpoises also have a strong instinct for community, whether gathering in herds by the thousands or traveling with only a few of their relatives, dolphin and porpoise herds travel together for life.

For all of their similarities, they are still separate species. Thinking of dolphins and porpoises as essentially the same beast is like comparing great apes to chimpanzees. They possess similar biological characteristics, but their appearance differs according to genetics, and their life-styles differ as a result of their habitats and survival needs.

In seas and rivers, dolphins and porpoises classified in the same family may live oceans away from each other and possess as many differences among them as humans do on earth. In a sense, the differences between species of dolphins and porpoises can be compared to racial differences in humans. A species found in one ocean may very likely have cousins in another. Atlantic and Pacific white-sided dolphins, for example, are two species within the same genus whose only real distinguishing characteristic is their coloration.

We shape our basic knowledge of dolphins and porpoises by their looks: size, shape, and color. Dolphins are noted for their beaks, which extend from below their foreheads, and for their conical teeth. Porpoise teeth, on the other hand, are flattened somewhat, and their rounded heads have no distinct beak. The

©James D. Watt

©Pieter A. Folkens

fins of dolphins and porpoises vary in size and shape, but on the whole dolphin fins are slightly larger proportionally than porpoise fins. Porpoise fins also are more triangular and less falcate than dolphin fins, though some porpoises have no dorsal fin at all. The concave trailing edge of dolphin fins immediately differentiates them from their porpoise cousins. The shape and size of dolphin and porpoise flippers also help distinguish between them. The most marked difference appears in the river dolphins, whose flippers are wide but with tips not as rounded as other cetaceans'. While all cetaceans have five "finger" bones that are webbed together in the flipper, river dolphins, unlike other dolphins, have flippers with a nubbed appearance, the bones not smoothly encased. Coloring and external markings are another key to identifying individual dolphins and porpoises.

In Chapter Three we discussed the basic biological characteristics of the odontocetes that suit them to their aquatic lifestyle. Beyond that, the Delphinidae, Phocoenidae, and Platanistidae evolved distinguishing biological and behavioral mechanisms to suit their own specific environments.

S*potted dolphins* (opposite page), *among the most social of all members of Delphinidae, swim together in large herds.* Above: *The dorsal fin of the Pacific white-sided dolphin is especially falcate, a concavity appearing on the posterior edge.*

R ight: *Here, two spotted dolphins break the surface to breathe. Though they often travel in large herds, spotted dolphins, like other members of the dolphin family, often swim in pairs.*

T he common dolphin, Delphinus delphis, *(opposite page) offers a striking example of the quick, smooth motion most odontocetes' streamlined bodies cut through the water.*

©James D. Watt

DOLPHINS *(DELPHINIDAE)*

Members of the family Delphinidae are the cetaceans most of us think of when the word "dolphin" is mentioned. Flipper, the famous dolphin of the television show of the 1960s, was a member of this group, as are many of the cetaceans who entertain spectators at oceanariums and aquariums. All members of the Delphinidae are not dolphins, however. Delphinidae is further divided in two subfamilies, Delphininae and Globicephalinae. Globicephalinae includes pilot whales (*Globicephala melaena*), killer whales (*Orcinus orca*), and Risso's dolphins (*Grampus griseus*). Killer whales inhabit the oceans all over the world up to ten to fifteen degrees from the poles, while their smaller dolphin relatives generally inhabit tropical, subtropical, and temperate waters. Delphininae encompasses at least thirty different species, and many genera are constantly being reclassified as more information is gathered about them and their relation to each other. In addition to *Stenella*, the dolphin family tree includes common dolphins (*Delphinus delphis*) and bottlenose dolphins (*Tursiops*), *Lagenorhynchus* (Atlantic and Pacific white-sided dolphins) and *Sousa* (hump-backed dolphins), *Lissodelphis,* and *Cephalorynchus* (among them Heaviside's dolphins).

GLOBICEPHALINAE

Killer Whales
(Orcinus orca)

S*wimming together in familial groups called pods, individual killer whales are distinguished by differences in their prominent white eye patches and gray "saddles" behind their dorsal fins.*

From its name, it doesn't take long to surmise the reputation killer whales have earned at sea. Sometimes known as *Orcas*, from the Anglo-Saxon word for "swordfish," killer whales earned their popular name from Basque whalers in the fifteenth century. The whalers named them "whale assassins," *Balaena assasina*, because they were known to attack and kill Northern right whales. The largest of the Delphinidae (growing up to thirty feet [nine meters] long and weighing as much as eight tons), they are also the most deadly predators next to humans, hunting even members of the whale order. Traveling in pods of up to 100 or

©Pieter A. Folkens

©Pieter A. Folkens

*T*his killer whale is "spy hopping," extending its

flippers to help it remain upright a little while longer.

more, killer whales are among the sea's most efficient hunters, working together to track down and devour their prey. (In fact, killer whales are the only known predators of blue whales, the largest of all cetaceans, and the arctic-dwelling leopard seal.)

The killer whale's tall dorsal fin, which stands out prominently when the animal skims the surface, its broad flippers, and its black-and-white markings distinguish it from smaller Delphinidae species such as Heaviside's dolphin, which has similar coloration. The killer whale's beak is not as pronounced as that of many other members of the dolphin family, but its straight mouth line houses four rows each of ten to twelve sharp teeth.

Killer whales are among the most easily trained of all the whales (see page 114), and, while some observers maintain that they survive in captivity for long periods of time, conservationists point out that stillborn killer whales are not counted, making the statistics on their longevity questionable. The striking patterns on its skin, the white marking behind and above the eye,

contrasting with its black back and its white chin and undersides, as well as its "playful" antics at marine parks makes the killer whale something of an imposter. They seem to be harmless showpieces to spectators, but in their natural environs they behave as any other carnivorous creature struggling for survival. Sometimes, however, killer whales do exhibit aggressive behavior in captivity. In one instance a dominant killer whale was transferred from Marineland of the Pacific to Sea World in San Diego. Living with new killer whales, it became upset and attacked one of its trainers.

Killer whales belong to their own subfamily, Globicephalinae, and differ slightly in appearance from region to region. The killer whales living closer to the poles have subtle differences from killer whales who live in tropical zones. Their distinctive markings—a gray patch on the saddle, the area behind the dorsal fin, and the white markings on their undersides and the white patch behind each eye—vary from individual to individual.

©Robert Pitman/EarthViews

These two photographs reveal the distinguishing feature of Risso's dolphins: The animals' gray epidermis is sensitive, resulting in white scratch marks.

©Marc Webber

Risso's Dolphin
(Grampus griseus)

Another member of the subfamily Globicephalinae, Risso's dolphin is similar to pilot whales and monodonts with its squared off, rounded forehead. It has no distinct beak, but a V-shaped crease on its forehead can be seen at close range. Part of its taxonomic name, *griseus*, derives from the Latin for "gray," referring to its coloring, though its dorsal fin, flukes, and flippers are darker. Scars appear all over its body, a result of its fragile epidermis, leading some to note that they look "as though a bucket of white paint has been spilled on them." In comparison to its thick, short body (it grows to a maximum length of between ten and thirteen feet [three and four meters]), its flippers and dorsal fin appear long and slender. It has no upper teeth, unlike other dolphin species, and its seven pairs of peglike teeth in the lower jaw are blunt and worn. In older animals they are often missing altogether.

Risso's dolphin has not been hunted, so study of them is not as complete as other species that are either hunted or aid in commercial fishing. One Risso's dolphin, named Pelorus Jack by his admirers around Cook Strait in New Zealand, would swim alongside ships moving through the strait. Famous throughout the world for his antics between 1888 and 1912, this playful dolphin appears in the writings of both Rudyard Kipling and Mark Twain.

We do know that Risso's dolphins like deep water in warm, tropical climates from Newfoundland to the Mediterranean and the Atlantic Ocean as far south as Argentina. In the Pacific Ocean they are found from Alaska to New Zealand and Australia. The "echelon" formation that groups of Risso's dolphins swim in is thought to be a hunting tactic, though further study may prove otherwise.

DELPHININAE

Common Dolphin
(Delphinus delphis)

The common, or saddleback, dolphin has the long, slim beak and streamlined body that most people imagine when they think of dolphins. Perhaps the most famous of all dolphins, *Delphinus delphis* appear in the frescoes at the Cretan Palace of Knossos, and are the dolphins whose form Apollo took when establishing his oracle at Delphi (see page 12).

Traveling in groups of up to a thousand and known for riding the waves of boats at sea, they are among the most sighted of all the dolphins, especially in the eastern North Pacific where they calve in the spring and fall. They also leap frequently into the air, giving them a reputation for being acrobats, though they have not survived in captivity to entertain at marine shows.

Common dolphins prefer deep waters far offshore in all oceans from the Pacific to the Atlantic in fairly warm latitudes. Able to dive to 925 feet (280 meters) and remain submerged for up to eight minutes, they feed on squid and fish and, off Southern California, on anchovies, smelt, and lantern fish. Like the bot-

tlenose dolphin (and other cetaceans), they will feed on the fish discarded from fishing boats.

Common dolphins' dorsal fin and facial patterns are highly variable, depending on their habitat. The pigmentation patterns range from the Atlantic species who boast bright orange patches on their sides to the Pacific species whose coloring is a dull gray. Nine separate variations on the stripe patterns also have been noted; sometimes the dolphin's face is light with little striping or is darker, with starkly contrasting stripes. Some subspecies may possess only one distinguishing stripe, which runs from underneath the eye to the flipper, while others will have as many as four. And, depending upon their region, their dorsal fins may be all black or they may be entirely white. Similar in appearance to spinner dolphins, many taxonomists question the separate classification of common and spinner dolphins. Only further study will show if these two groups will one day be considered members of the same genus.

©C. Allan Morgan

©Marc Webber/EarthViews

Spinner Dolphin
(Stenella spp.)

Like the common dolphin, spinners have long, dark beaks and slim, tapered bodies. Their common name derives from their habit of leaping and spinning in the air. Currently, the genus *Stenella*, of which there are many species—among them the Costa Rican spinner, eastern spinner, whitebelly spinner, Hawaiian spinner, and short-snout spinner—is being reevaluated by taxonomists and it could take years before final conclusions are reached about the classification of this vast group of dolphins.

The concern of the National Marine Fisheries Service over the effect purse-seine fishing has on the spinner-dolphin population makes this genus one of the most studied of the oceanic dolphin groups. Their bond with the yellowfin, or light-meat, tuna has placed their population in danger (see pages 123 to 127) as thousands are caught or injured in tuna-fishing nets each year.

Opposite page: *Displaying its "saddleback" stripe, but trying to lose its new traveling companion, a common dolphin leaps, revealing the remora stuck to its side.* Above: *Often seen swimming in pairs, spinner dolphins are named for their frequent spins as they leap into the air. Commonly sighted in the Eastern Tropical Pacific, they face serious population depletion as a result of purse-seine fishing practices.*

Bottlenose Dolphin
(Tursiops)

Residents of all warm-temperate to tropical oceans except in high latitudes, the two varieties of bottlenose dolphins—coastal and offshore species—are among the most playful of the dolphin family. Taxonomists sometimes split this group into three subspecies—*Tursiops truncatus truncatus* (Atlantic Ocean), *T. truncatus aduncus* (Indian Ocean, Australia), and *T. truncatus gilli* (pelagic Pacific)—based on their size differences: *T. truncatus truncatus* are up to fifteen feet (five meters) long, *T. truncatus aduncus* are ten to twelve feet (four meters)long, while the smallest, *T. truncatus gilli* are about eight feet (2.4 meters) long. Bottlenose dolphins often swim along the bows of fishing boats and play in their wakes, which in some areas has done them more harm than good. Frustrated fishermen have shot at them when they get caught in their nets, and many are in captivity in zoos and aquariums. Nonetheless, bottlenose dolphins continue to seek out the company of humans at sea and often allow themselves to be touched and petted.

Their attraction to humans doesn't stop at mere playfulness. Feeding naturally on fish, invertebrates, and sometimes squid, bottlenose dolphins have been known to eat fish thrown away by fishing boats and to feed on the fish that gather around fishing boats. Without this "help" from humans, bottlenose dolphins seem, like killer whales, to hunt together using their communicative squeaks and clicks to lead them to the feast. The average

group of twenty-five offshore bottlenose dolphins is slightly larger than groups of their coastal counterparts, who travel in groups of ten or less. Coastal varieties sometimes flip over on their backs, feeding upside down to maximize echolocation.

Most bottlenose dolphins grow to an adult length of about thirteen feet (four meters) and are dark or charcoal gray, though some appear lighter gray or brown and may have spots on their bodies. While all bottlenose dolphins have a short beak that clearly juts from the head, each type has a slightly different body shape. Most have a thick head and body that tapers to the flukes beginning behind their dorsal fin. However, much thinner bottlenose dolphins have been seen.

*T*he dolphin known as "Flipper" to prime-time TV viewers of the 1960s had a winning smile and a congenial personality, not unlike his ocean-roaming relatives. Though the smile is an aquadynamic feature that helps the dolphin swim more quickly through water, it does make some people want to flash a grin in return.

©Gerard Wellington/EarthViers

Pacific and Atlantic White-Sided Dolphins, Dusky Dolphins, and Hourglass Dolphins *(Lagenorhynchus)*

Unlike any other genus of marine mammals, *Lagenorhynchus* has the distinction of being the only one in which separate speciation has occurred in all the major subpolar oceans. Species of *Lagenorhynchus* are found in the North and South Pacific, the North and South Atlantic, and in the Indian Ocean. While speciation within the genus *Stenella*, for example, led to comparable Atlantic and Pacific ocean species, only in *Lagenorhynchus* have scientists identified counterpart species in each ocean.

Although Pacific and Atlantic white-sided dolphins (*L. obliquidens* and *L. acutus*) live in different oceans, as co-members of a fixed member genus they bear the same descriptive name and fill a similar environmental niche. Each species of *Lagenorhynchus* evolved isolated in its own habitat. The Atlantic dolphin inhabits the northern North Atlantic ocean from Britain to Cape Cod and the Baltic and North Seas; the Pacific dolphins evolved in the more temperate waters of the Pacific Ocean north of the tropics and south of the colder Arctic Sea. While the Atlantic white-sided dolphin's coloring runs from black or gray on its back to a white belly with tan or yellow markings on its sides, its Pacific cousin has a black back with gray sides and a bright white ventral side.

The *Lagenorhynchus* dolphins have similar body shapes, but there are subtle differences between them. While the Atlantic dolphin's gently sloped forehead ends abruptly at a deep crease, marking the beginning of its snout, the Pacific dolphin's snout can clearly can be distinguished from its forehead, but it doesn't start so abruptly. Pacific dolphins have from twenty-one to twenty-eight teeth, while the Atlantic dolphin possesses between thirty and forty.

Both white-sided dolphins are noted for their falcate dorsal fins, though the Pacific's dorsal fin appears almost hooked at the top. This distinction has earned it the name "hooked-fin porpoise," a misnomer both because its fin isn't really hooked and, of course, because it belongs to the dolphin family.

As with most dolphins, members of *Lagenorhynchus* are gregarious. Their herding behavior is an evolutionary adaptation that gives them a distinct advantage in their environment. Swimming in herds, dolphins have the advantage of protection in numbers, sharing the rearing of young, and more effective hunting techniques. All of these evolutionary selections so far have been successful for them (see page 79 for more on these

T*he dusky dolphin* (left), *is known for its acrobatic*

ability. Even so, the Atlantic white-sided dolphin (below)

offers its share of acrobatic leaps.

©Marc Webber

©Pieter A. Folkens

Like its Pacific white-sided dolphin counterpart, the

dusky dolphin (left) displays its leaps and spins at every

opportunity. The Pacific white-sided and dusky dolphins are

very similar in appearance. Above: Little is known about the

hourglass dolphin, another of the Lagenorhynchus genus,

because it resides in the seldom traveled waters of the high

latitudes of the southern hemisphere.

evolutionary advantages in "Community Living"). While the Atlantic white-sided dolphin may travel close to shore in small groups of six to eight during the summer, more often it has been sighted farther out to sea in groups as large as 700; the Pacific dolphin has been sighted in herds of a thousand or more. For both dolphins, groups of 100 or more are more common.

Pacific white-sided dolphins are noted for their frequent leaps. While the uneducated observer might interpret this as evidence of the dolphin's gregariousness and playfulness, some experts believe that leaping may actually conserve energy for the dolphin and help them move along more quickly.

Other species in the *Lagenorhynchus* genus is the dusky dolphin (*L. obscurus*), the equally acrobatic Southern Hemisphere counterpart to the Northern Hemisphere Pacific white-sided dolphin. With markings like those of Pacific white-sided dolphins but with slightly lighter coloring, dusky and Pacific white-sided dolphins share evolutionary characteristics. Scientists don't understand as much about two other species within *Lagenorhynchus*—the Southern Hemisphere Peale's dolphin (*L. australis*) and the hourglass dolphin (*L. cruciger*)—known to exist only in the southernmost Antarctic waters, where they are not seen often because they inhabit an area not populated by many people. Based on skull study, all species of this remarkable genus possess many evolutionary similarities.

©Pieter A. Folkens

Northern Right Whale Dolphin
(Lissodelphis)

Unlike any of its delphininae cousins, the northern right whale dolphin has no dorsal fin gracing its slim, dark body. Aquiline and graceful, their flippers and flukes are slender. The highest population of dolphins living in the temperate North Pacific, *Lissodelphis borealis* seldom ventures into the tropics or north to arctic waters. Though they are highly social, sometimes traveling in large herds of 1,000 or more, they usually avoid boats and contact with humans. Even so, they often are the victims of Japanese gill-net and purse-seine fishing. When they can escape boats and their nets, they skillfully swim away, just breaking the surface with their blowholes to breathe. Having no dorsal fins and a deep black color, they are hard to spot.

Heaviside's and Commerson's Dolphins
(Cephalorhynchus)

Smaller than most dolphins, little is known about these two members of the genus *Cephalorhynchus*. Their name derives from the Greek word for head, *kephale,* and *rhyncos,* meaning "snout," referring to their long rostrums. They have small beaks and low dorsal fins and rounded flippers that more closely resemble porpoise fins than dolphin fins. Their coastal habitats and the sounds they make also link them to porpoises.

Heaviside's dolphin (*C. heavisidii*) is generally found off the southwestern coast of Africa, while Commerson's dolphin (*C. commersonii*) resides in the waters of the southern Indian Ocean and in the South Atlantic Ocean off the coast of southern South America.

*T*he fin of the Commerson's dolphin (opposite page) is smaller and more rounded than those of other dolphins. Left: The finless figure of the northern right whale dolphin strikes a graceful pose against the blue ocean.

RIVER DOLPHINS (PLATANISTIDAE)

The river dolphins have historically been lumped in the family Platanistidae. Further study has lead taxonomists and paleontologists to regroup them into four subfamilies—Platanistidae, Inidae, Lipotidae and Pontoporidae. Two of the species of Platanista, Indus Susu and Ganges Susu, are so similar that taxonomists often group them together, yet more often than not they are considered to be one species. Platanista and Inia have the distinction of being the only freshwater species within the order Cetacea, Lipotidae is an estuarine species, and Pontoporidae actually is a coastal oceanic species. The five species of river dolphin inhabit the Yangtze River in China, the Ganges and Indus Rivers in India, and the Amazon River and coastal waters of South America.

The unusual skulls and rostrums of the river dolphins are more analogous to known prehistoric species than to any other living species in Delphinidae. Their long, narrow beaks and jaws holding hundreds of teeth are unlike any of the other toothed whales. Consequently, their flukes are larger than oceanic dolphins and they swim more slowly than their saltwater counterparts. Scientists point out that in their river habitat they evolved more power than speed, as life is generally slower in the limited space available in the rivers. They also breathe more often than many of the Delphinidae, and, with the exception of the Franciscana dolphin, have straight slits for blowholes rather than a crescent-shaped slit. Some species have very poor eyesight—the Ganges and Indus River dolphins being the only marine mammals whose eyes do not have lenses—and would be functionally blind if not for echolocation. Another factor paleontologists cite in linking them to primitive dolphins are their flexible necks.

PLATANISTIDAE

Ganges Susu and Indus Susu
(P. gangetica and P. minor)

Taxonomists still disagree over considering these dolphins as separate species. Though they live in different areas and exhibit slightly different skull morphology, they are very similar in appearance. Both hardy swimmers, the Ganges and Indus river dolphins battle the strong river currents unlike any of the other species in their family. They appear to swim with a side-to-side motion, but they actually turn on their sides to facilitate the use of echolocation. While some dolphins will roll on their sides while swimming, this phenomenon is a regular feature in the Ganges and Indus river dolphins' repertoire. Even in shallow waters, these small, chunky animals turn on their side, using one of their flippers to help propel them by pushing off from the riverbed. The only dolphins without crystalline eye lenses and with eye openings about the size of a pinhole, many believe the Susus are blind even to light. Because of their eye-size, these dolphins depend solely on echolocation to find food.

Uncharacteristic of its river cousins, the Susus will lift their bodies above the water, often falling over backward and slapping their tails against the surface. Since this seems to happen in rough waters or when the dolphin's environs are intruded upon by boats, scientists believe this may be a distress signal to other dolphins, rather than "playful" acrobatics as it appears in other cetaceans.

Like their river-dwelling relatives, these dolphins remain submerged only for short periods of time, at most thirty to forty-five seconds, and feed at night on catfish, shrimp, and crabs. Their sharp teeth and long beaks, extending at a sharp angle from their small skulls, allow them to catch prey as much as a foot (thirty-five centimeters) long.

The Susus have adapted to their river environment, following its tides just as their oceanic counterparts sense the rising and falling tides of the sea. During the rainy season, they often swim into tributaries searching for food and return to the river just before the monsoon season ends.

A distinguishing characteristic of the Indus Susu is its habit of swimming in counterclockwise circles. It moves constantly, slowing its movement only when feeding or when the barometric pressure drops because of an impending storm. Its blowhole is placed to the left of center of its head. When it breaks the surface to breathe, it rolls slightly to the right, a ridge along the right side of its blowhole protecting it from the water.

The Indus Susu, like many other of the dolphin families, is in danger of extinction due to the intrusion of human industry along the river. Dams built for irrigation have interfered with their migration habits and divided members of their herds. While they once were plentiful, inhabiting the entire length of the Indus River system, today they can only be found between Sukkur and Taunsa in Pakistan.

LIPOTIDAE

Beiji
(Lipotes vexillifer)

The Yangtze River in China has been home to this dolphin for at least as long as Chinese recorded history. Unfortunately, it is also among the most endangered species of dolphins—efforts to save the species have come too infrequently and, some believe, too late to save it. Often referred to as the Yangtze River Dolphin (*Lipotes vexillifer*), it is less commonly called the "white flag" dolphin, which derives from a mistranslation of the Sufi word *fer*, which means "carry, bear."

Like other river dolphins, the Beiji swims slowly, surfaces every forty seconds, and depends on its ability to echolocate to maneuver. Seeing a Beiji's flukes is rare; they are difficult to approach and when the dolphin dives to get away from boats and people, it moves without breaking the surface. In most dolphin species the eyes are placed at the sides of its head, just above and behind the mouth. The Beiji's eyes, on the other hand are placed near the top of its head, and its large ear openings appear where the eyes are in other members of the Delphinidae. Though other cetaceans' blowholes may be to the left of center of their heads, the right side of the Beiji's skull is exaggerated unlike any other dolphin.

Like other river dolphins, the Beiji travel in small groups of two to six and feed only at night. Unlike their relatives, they are not gregarious. Their thirty to thirty-four evenly sized, peglike teeth are housed in a long, narrow beak that turns up slightly at the tip. The shape of the beak may help them dig for food on the river floor.

T*he Indus River dolphin's beak and teeth seem*

almost prehistoric. Because it lives in a very muddy environ-

ment it has adapted a pinhole for an eye opening and relies

solely on echolocation to maneuver and hunt.

©Ted Stephenson/EarthViews

INIDAE

Boutu
(Inia geoffrensis)

The Boutu takes full advantage of its changing habitat, swimming to the flow of the rising and falling river as its Asian cousins do. As the river rises and floods the nearby forest, the dolphins follow the fish that swim into this "new" area of the river. When the water recedes after a few days, the fish remain while the dolphins swim safely back to the deeper waters of the main part of the river. Another environmental adaptation is its skin color. At birth, Boutus are slate blue but darken as they mature. Depending on the waters they inhabit, however, their skin color seems to darken more or less according to the clarity of the water. Residents of the Negro and Japurá Rivers, the darkest of all, are brightly colored, while the inhabitants of the Tapajoz, a clear river, exhibit the darkest pigmentation of all the Inia species.

Though residing in another hemisphere, the Boutu shares some common characteristics with the Beiji and Susu dolphins: its blowhole is to the left of center of its head, and the Boutu shares the shy and retiring disposition of the Susu, breaking the surface of the water with only its melon and blowhole. One distinguishing characteristic of the Boutu, however, is that its forehead is thicker and more bulbous than the other river dolphins. While the Susu's beak is proportionally longer than any other dolphin's, often being one-third of its body length, the actual measure of the Boutu's beak is longer than that of the Beiji or Susu.

Like the Platanistas, the Boutu feeds on catfish. Unlike any other cetacean species, it chews its food: with its sharp, pointed front teeth it tears into its prey and chews on the tough skin of the catfish with its molarlike rear teeth. Another unique adaptation of this species are the bristles on its lower jaw and upper beak. With these, the Boutu dolphin is better able to nudge crustaceans off the river's floor. Sometimes it even swims upside down to dig food out of the riverbed with its beak.

PONTOPORIDAE

Franciscana
(Pontoporia blainvillei)

Traditionally classified in the family Platanistidae, Pontoporia represents a good example of the need to reorganize the family into four separate groups. Though the Franciscana resembles the other river dolphins with its long, slender beak, unlike the other Platanistas, it is not a freshwater dolphin. A resident of the coastal ocean off the coasts of Uruguay and Argentina, it is sometimes referred to as an estuarine species, because it swims into lagoons to feed. Its crescent-shaped blowhole also distinguishes it from its river relatives. The shape of its beak and jaw, like other river dolphins, allows it to dig into the ocean floor for its diet of octopus and crustaceans. With over 240 teeth, it has more than any other species of dolphin.

©Connie Ewald

©Ken Balcomb/EarthViews

PORPOISES (PHOCOENIDAE)

With small, triangular dorsal fins and little or no beak at all, members of the family Phocoenidae are, contrary to popular terminology, the only true porpoises. On the whole, porpoises are smaller and appear chubbier than dolphins, because of their less exaggerated dorsal fins. Their teeth are flatter than dolphin teeth and their fins are often slightly smaller and more triangular than those of the dolphins. The largest porpoise, the spectacled porpoise, measures just over six feet (about two meters) long, though the average size for porpoises is between four and a half and six feet (one and two meters). The largest of the Delphinidae, on the other hand, measure thirty feet (nine meters) while most measure just over six feet (two meters). Porpoises also tend to travel in smaller groups than most dolphins. Though some have been sighted in groups of up to fifty, most prefer to travel with ten

T*he small, chubby harbor porpoise* (opposite page) *has a triangular dorsal fin that distinguishes all porpoises (except for the finless porpoise) from dolphins.* Above: *Among the largest of the porpoises, Dall's porpoise often falls prey to deadly killer whales.*

or fewer companions. The harbor, or common, porpoise (*Phocoena phocoena*), Burmeister's porpoise (*P. spinipinnis*), the spectacled porpoise (*P. dioptrica*), the finless porpoise (*Neophocaena phocoenoides*), Dall's porpoise (*P. dalli*), and the Cochito, or Vaquita, (*P. sinus*) are the six species that have been identified since the first harbor porpoise was classified, in 1758.

Burmeister's Porpoise
(Phocoena spinipinnis)

Little is known about this small porpoise. Scientists do know that Burmeister's inhabits the shallow, coastal waters of South America. The few that have been studied have been caught accidentally in fishing nets or purposefully for bait and food. Some 2,000 Burmeister's porpoises were reportedly sold in Peru in one year.

Its distinctive feature is the convex shape of the rear edge of its dorsal fin; the trailing edge of all other dolphins and porpoises is concave. Save for variations in its color and its few teeth (it has only about sixty), Burmeister's porpoise is similar to the harbor porpoise in all other respects.

Cochito
(Phocoena sinus)

The Cochito is a porpoise measuring about four and a half feet (one and a third meters). It is similar in appearance to the common porpoise, but the proportions of its skull and skeleton are closer to those of Burmeister's porpoise. Its back is medium to dark gray, its undersides are white, and it has a small, triangular dorsal fin. Though little is known of this species, scientists theorize that they move north to south with the seasons and feed on Gulf croakers and squid.

An inhabitant of the Gulf of California, the Cochito is an endangered species discovered in 1958 by noted cetacean expert Kenneth Norris. (For more on Norris and his research, see pages 89–90, 100, and 113–115).

Conservationists argue that the damming of the Colorado River and the dumping of toxic waste in the upper Gulf inhibit the Cochito's ability to restock its population. Only recently has a Cochito been seen alive or, if dead, in a fresh enough condition to study. The few that still survive today are threatened by gill-net fisheries.

©Ken Balcomb/EarthViews

Harbor Porpoise
(Phocoena phocoena)

This chubby representative of the porpoise family grows to a maximum length of only about five feet (about one and a half meters). It has a flat snout, a beak that is not strongly demarcated, and a round body that weighs as much as 130 pounds (fifty-nine kilograms). A plump little creature that, when poked, will squeal like a pig, it's no wonder the Romans called them *porcus piscus*, or pigfish. Today, they are often sighted in the Bay of Fundy, and Canadians call them puffing pigs. They have dark brown or gray backs and grayish-brown sides and dive for short periods of time, surfacing six to eight times a minute.

Residents of coastal regions and bays in cold temperate waters of the Northern Hemisphere, harbor porpoises feed on fish that swim in schools, such as herring, mackerel, sardines, and pollack. Although they swim playfully in front of each other, whole groups circling each other when they meet in the ocean, they are wary of boats and humans. Most harbor-porpoise populations are still abundant, but heavy fishing in the Black Sea and the Baltic Sea has brought their numbers here dangerously low.

T*hough often sighted in harbors off the east coast of Canada, the harbor porpoise* (opposite page) *faces many of the dangers confronting other marine mammals: Pollutants and irresponsible fishing practices threaten its health and survival. Also known as the Vaquita, the Cochito porpoise* (below) *population is endangered.*

©Robert Pitman/EarthViews

Finless Porpoise
(Neophocaena phocaenoides)

Like the *Lissodelphis* dolphin, this anomalous species of the porpoise family has no dorsal fin at all. Unlike other porpoises, however, it does have the suggestion of a beak, which protrudes beneath its broad, square forehead. Gray all over, with slight blue coloring on the back and sides, this porpoise might be confused with the beluga whale by the uninitiated. Traveling in subgroups of two to twelve, finless porpoises have been sighted in groups as large as fifty in the coastal waters of the Indo-Pacific. They also inhabit the Yangtze River.

While little is known about their mating and nurturing habits, calves have been observed hanging on to little bumps on their mothers' backs, hitching a ride whenever they can.

Dall's Porpoise
(Phocoena dalli)

Sometimes called the "spray" porpoise, Dall's porpoises are the stockiest, yet fastest, of all the porpoises. Famous for the "rooster tail," a stream of water that arcs up and over them when they surface, they do not leap. As they swim toward the surface to breathe, the stocky shape of their head and shoulders creates a vortex around the top of their heads; just before they surface, they exhale a bit, which creates a cone of air around their blowhole, spraying water behind them. This ingenious method of breathing allows them to swim faster than they would if they had to break the surface to breathe.

Growing to a length of seven feet (about two and a half meters), they weigh as much as 480 pounds (218 kilograms). With their black-and-white coloring and triangular dorsal fins, they might be mistaken for killer whales when in their vicinity at sea. Naturalists Pieter Folkens and Steve Cooper have dubbed Dall's porpoises "killer whale larvae," because, despite their size, their proximity to killer whales indicates that they are about to become the orcas' dinner.

Unlike other porpoises, Dall's porpoises have been known to swim alongside boats and ride their bow or stern waves. Their sociability is a concern to conservationists, however, as many have been killed by Japanese gill- and drift-net fishing.

Feeding on squid, crustaceans, and fish such as herring and hake, Dall's porpoises reside in the northern Pacific Ocean and the southern Bering Sea in deep waters and are often sighted off the Puget Sound closer to shore. To grasp their slippery prey, they have a row of "gum teeth" that surround their normal teeth.

©Ken Balcomb/EarthViews

Like the northern right whale dolphin, the finless porpoise, through evolution, has lost its dorsal fin. A highly social porpoise, it is often sighted in groups of twelve to fifty, and with other species such as Risso's dolphin and the Pacific white-sided dolphin.

Spectacled Porpoise
(Phocoena dioptrica)

Named for the heavy black rim around its eyes, which resembles eyeglasses, the spectacled porpoise is the Southern Hemisphere equivalent of the Northern Hemisphere Dall's porpoise. Though it was identified in 1912, only ten of the animals had been sighted until the mid-1970s. Not until 1978, when over 100 were beached at Tierra del Fuego, were they studied in large numbers.

Even so, we do know that the coloring of the spectacled porpoise distinguishes it from its South American cousin, Burmeister's porpoise. From the top of its snout, along the line of its eye almost to its flukes, its back is black. Below that line, the porpoise is white or gray, with flippers that are white with a gray border and dark flukes. Unlike other porpoises and dolphins, the tip of its dorsal fin is slightly rounded. Believed to be the largest of the porpoises, the spectacled porpoise measures about six feet (just over two meters) long.

A*lthough the distinctive black-and-white body of Dall's porpoise is chunky, the mammal is a fast swimmer and often will ride the bow or stern waves of boats.*

©Robert Pitman/Earth Views

Chapter Five
Community Living

Legendary for their playfulness and curiosity, the sociability of dolphins and porpoises—with humans, with each other, and with other marine mammals—has been the subject of debate and controversy since Aristotle first recorded dolphin-human interaction. Traveling in herds ranging from two to 2,000, the odontocetes' social reputation has more to do with their hunting and reproduction requirements than with their innate "friendliness": their complex social order is simply another adaptation to their environment for survival. As discussed in Chapter Three, dolphins and porpoises adapted certain biological and physiological specializations to hunt their prey. Their jaw shape and teeth (see page 46) facilitate catching their food, but their social behavior, ability to emit sounds, and echolocation serve to track, locate, and, recent studies show, actually stun their prey.

Closely linked to these specializations that nature has ingeniously endowed the odontocetes with are their mating and migration habits. As with any animal, they need food to maintain their metabolic rate; without it, mating, bearing, and nurturing their young would be next to impossible. These fundamental survival requirements—food and the ability to reproduce—necessitated the evolution of an intricate social network among dolphins and porpoises, which has led cetacean author Richard Ellis to observe that they have some sort of "instinctive compassion." Other researchers point out that this care-giving behavior is a characteristic of all mammals and is further necessitated by the dolphins' aquatic environment.

THE SOCIAL CONNECTION

Most dolphins and porpoises depend on others of their species for survival, whether they roam the ocean in groups of three or numbers reaching into the thousands. Studies of bottlenose dolphins in Argentina and Florida, spinner dolphins in Hawaii, harbor porpoises in Canada, white-beaked and Risso's dolphins in North Scotland, and captive dolphins and porpoises show that traveling in groups supports their hunting strategy, serves as protection from predators, and facilitates mating and raising their young. Primarily predators of fish and squid, dolphins and porpoises find their food sources using echolocation (see page 84). Exploiting their food source also is facilitated by herding behavior—inshore species traveling in smaller groups, the pelagic species hunting and socializing in larger groups.

While researchers believe that all species of dolphins and porpoises rely on echolocation to hunt and to aid in maintaining their social bonds, not all dolphins emit the same sounds or travel in the same kinds of groups. The pelagic species such as common, spinner, and spotted dolphins, which feed on schooling fish, hunt by traveling in large groups, allowing them to cover a

*K*iller whales are extremely social animals, a quality that makes them effective hunters. Here, killer whales spy hop together in Blackfish Sound, British Columbia.

wider area and to rely on each other to find the most bountiful feeding areas. The inshore species such as the porpoises and the bottlenose dolphin tend to form smaller herds—their prey don't travel in large herds. Dolphin herds are only as large as the food source can support.

With some species, the size and composition of a herd varies from region to region and, sometimes, from hour to hour. While observers note that the mother-calf bond forms the base for odontocete social behavior (see page 90, "Mating and Nurturing"), their overall herding behavior is most often described as "fluid." Bernd Wursig, who studied the behavior of bottlenose dolphins extensively in Argentina, notes that offshore herds of thirty to fifty animals congregated only when there was a large amount of herring in the area. His studies also showed that while a core group would stay in one area for a long period of time, many individuals would leave for as long as a few weeks, then return; others would leave and never return.

Killer whales, on the other hand, have a strict social order. Traveling together in familial groups called pods—subsets of a herd composed of a female, her daughters, and their young, and an attending adult male who serves as a scout and protector—they maintain bonds with their relatives. Several pods will congregrate into a superpod in order to allow males to mate with females of other pods, providing a mixing of the gene pool.

©Pieter A. Folkens

©Philip Rosenberg

Dr. Randy Wells, of the University of California at Santa Cruz's Long Marine Lab, is following up his study of Hawaiian spinner and Florida bottlenose dolphin populations with analyses of dolphins' blood groups. Wells believes that just as people are related by blood ties, with members of one family possessing similar proteins and hormones, blood samples from a group of dolphins will tell us something about dolphins' own family ties. Three new tanks at the Long Marine Lab will accommodate a resident group of Pacific white-sided dolphins for Wells to study. Wells began his work in the field, where he photographed scores of bottlenose dolphins at Sarasota Bay, Florida. By studying the markings of the animals he photographed—notable scars on their backs or notches on their dorsal fins—and by tagging them, Wells concluded that bottlenose dolphins congregated in groups of females and calves; young males; and groups of older males.

The fluidity of odontocete congregations is confirmed by the sometimes wide variation in the sizes of the groups. Spotted-dolphin herds can range from twenty to 200 during the day and up to 2,500 when they feed at night. Coastal species such as the harbor porpoise, on the other hand, are seldom seen in congregations of more than three to five, and coastal bottlenose dolphin groups average about ten. David Gaskin points out that the fluctuations in the size of dolphin and porpoise herds is related to their "patchy and irregular food supply." Like nomadic plains animals, he says, "subunits [of dolphins] come together opportunistically into larger feeding aggregations when food is plentiful."

Just as military aircraft fly in formation, staggering the distance from each other above and below and from side to side, pelagic dolphins utilize similar formations to stalk their prey. Echelons of Hawaiian spinner dolphins, staggered both horizontally and vertically, sometimes spread over several miles. This formation may help them swim more efficiently while providing more room for their individual sonar capabilities to go to work. When they converge on a herd of fish to feed, however, they swim close together, frightening the fish to the surface (see page 86). Dusky dolphins in Argentina also seem to have an instinct for how their spatial relationship in the water will affect them: one group swam single file to avoid being seen by predators.

Regardless of a herd's size, its level of activity, or its location, all dolphins and porpoises rely on their ability to echolocate, emitting sounds to feed and to locate each other.

eft: *Typically traveling in large herds, spotted dolphins will often swim in an echelon to maximize their hunting strategy. Below: Killer whale pods are among the most efficient social and familial units in the sea. Killer whales naturally regulate their birth rate according to the carrying capacity and food supply of the environment. It is believed that they share mates between pods to maintain a mix in the gene pod.*

Echolocation and Communication

To achieve this level of hunting and feeding in an environment where seeing is difficult at best, dolphins and porpoises evolved a strong acoustic sense. Sound waves travel some five times faster in the water than in air, and the structure of the dolphin head suits it to finding prey acoustically, by echolocation. Kenneth Norris and his colleagues were the first to theorize that the melon—the waxy, lens-shaped substance in the forehead of odontocetes—directs the squeaks and clicks that the animals emit in a sonar beam, bouncing the sounds off objects and prey in their environment to "see" it. Dolphins create their clicks, whistles, and squeaks by pushing air from the nares to the vestibular nasal sacs. Some believe the whistles come from the left side of the head, the clicks from the right. This process is something like releasing air from a balloon by stretching its neck between your fingers and letting the air escape slowly. Another theory is that sounds produced in the larynx are emitted through the head. In either case, the echoes are received by the lower jaw and passed through oil there to the acoustic window, a membrane at the back of the jaw, and then to the ear bone. In the human ear, the cochlea vibrates, sending sound vibrations to nerve endings in the inner ear, which then pass the message along to the brain. In the same way, sounds vibrate through the acoustic window in the dolphin's jaw and are passed to nerve endings in its brain.

While cetacean experts agree that echolocation plays a big part in finding herds of fish and scanning the dolphins' terrain, they caution that calling these sounds "communication" means only that they are capable of transmitting signals, not of actually "talking" to each other. (For more on dolphin sounds and echolocation and their relation to communication and intelligence, see Chapter Six.) While the human ear can distinguish about thirty clicks per second, dolphins can distinguish some 700 sonar clicks per second. Bottlenose dolphins emit sounds at varying frequencies, from high-frequency clicking sounds (2.0 to 220 kHz), which are used to discriminate between objects in the ocean, to lower-frequency clicks (0.25 to 1.0 kHz), which are called "orientation clicks" and offer a more general picture of their surroundings. The frequency of the sounds changes according to the dolphin's activities—resting, feeding, or in response to danger from predators. Studies of killer whales in the Puget Sound reveal that each pod possesses its own set of sounds, much as the humpback whale develops its own pattern of "singing." Some theorize that the high-frequency echolocation sounds are used to navigate, while another set of unpulsed sounds, whistles, and squeaks (not found in some odontocetes, such as sperm whales, river dolphins, harbor porpoises, and Heaviside's dolphins) may help identify a particular group (as is the case of killer whale pods) as well as identify individuals by their sex, age, and level of activity. The pulsing click sounds travel farther than the unpulsed sounds, leading scientists to theorize that the short-range whistles and squeaks may be communication between animals.

In any case, echolocation in dolphins is highly accurate. In one test, a dolphin was able to distinguish between a ball of aluminum and a ball of tin that were the same size. This acute sonic ability to distinguish between the density of metals led the military to experiment with dolphins (see page 118).

We still have much to learn about echolocation, however. As *CMS News*, a publication of the University of California at Santa Cruz, explains, "If you can imagine yourself blind, at a party where everyone is speaking a language that you don't know, you will have an idea of what marine mammal researchers are up against." At the Long Marine Lab, Dr. Ken Marten hopes to unravel some of the mystery of echolocation by constructing a giant human head that will be used to listen to dolphin sounds both at the lab's tanks and at sea. Until now, researchers have not been able to tell which individual was making what sound. Using giant, reconstructed human ears equipped with hydrophones (underwater microphones), Marten will be able to analyze individual sounds made by dolphins according to their pitch and intensity, evaluating them by comparing the sounds to what the dolphins were doing at the time. To study dolphin sounds in their natural habitat, Marten hopes that placing three hydrophones underwater about fifty feet (fifteen meters) and another below those at 300 to 600 feet (100 to 200 meters), where a group has congregated, will give him a "three-dimensional" picture of the sounds. If all goes well, Marten will know from a videotape what the dolphin was doing and from his audio recording where the dolphin was and what sounds it made.

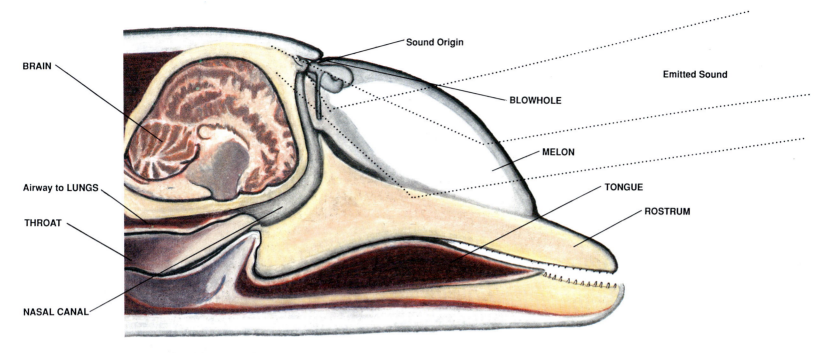

BRAIN

Airway to LUNGS

THROAT

NASAL CANAL

Sound Origin

BLOWHOLE

Emitted Sound

MELON

TONGUE

ROSTRUM

Figure A: Sound Transmission

Medial view of dolphin head.

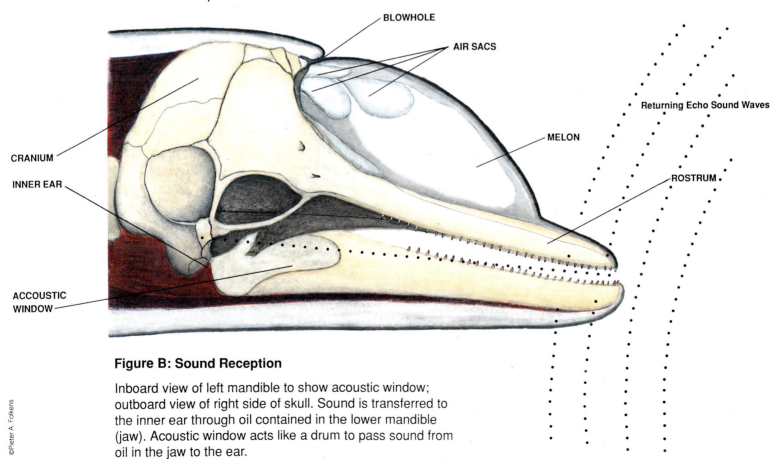

BLOWHOLE

AIR SACS

Returning Echo Sound Waves

MELON

CRANIUM

INNER EAR

ROSTRUM

ACCOUSTIC
WINDOW

Figure B: Sound Reception

Inboard view of left mandible to show acoustic window;
outboard view of right side of skull. Sound is transferred to
the inner ear through oil contained in the lower mandible
(jaw). Acoustic window acts like a drum to pass sound from
oil in the jaw to the ear.

Hunting and Herding

Dolphins' hunting prowess is indisputable, yet they rely on much more than their all-important echolocation to find their prey. Their playful leaps, breaches, spins, and fin and head slaps may in fact not be so playful at all: The activity and sounds created may be a signal to other dolphins that food for the taking is in the area. The sounds these movements create could also frighten their prey. Spotted, spinner, common, dusky, white-beaked, and bottlenose dolphins may also use echolocation to find a large school of fish. Once found, some of the dolphins swim below the schooling fish, circling around them and driving them toward the surface (the dolphins creating a ruckus all the while by flailing their bodies about), where the fish become trapped between the dolphins and the air. Recent studies by Ken Norris show that the repeated echo-clicks they emit while feeding help herd the fish together, perhaps even stunning them with their sonarlike beams.

Blasts of sound up to 230 decibels—about as loud as a jet engine and sounding something like a gunshot—were recorded in 1980. Since then, Ken Norris and his colleagues have theorized that some dolphins use these sounds to slow down the desired fish, while others stun their prey before moving in to eat. These loud sounds are of a lower frequency than the other clicks that dolphins emit and last about 1,000 times longer. The sound is powerful enough to paralyze the fish by damaging their lateral lines, an organ that detects variations in the water's pressure.

Closer to land, bottlenose dolphins off the west coast of Africa, Atlantic humpback dolphins, and harbor porpoises herd fish toward sloped, sandy shores. In the same way, killer whales, among the many odontocete species who make use of their great size to create a cacophony of sound, also slap the surface with their flippers or flukes, and squeak to herd salmon together and trap them between the shore and the tide. Killer whales use these sounds to herd their more intelligent prey of Dall's porpoises. In Madagascar, studies by Pieter Arend Folkens show that Indo-Pacific humpback dolphins herd fish toward a volcanic bench, a wall of lava. For this strategy to work, the dolphins wait until the tide is low enough to prevent their prey from swimming over the rock.

I

n this sequence captured by Pieter Folkens, a killer whale stalks and attacks a Dall's porpoise. In the first frame (opposite page, far left), *the killer whale slaps its flipper on the water to frighten the porpoise toward shore; in a "headout" position* (opposite page, left), *the killer whale then chases the porpoises; finally it leaps for its prey* (below) *and snatches it just below the surface of the water.*

©Pieter A. Folkens

Cooperation or Hidden Aggression?

Clearly, the tendency to group together at sea and near the shore (however small the groups may be) works to the advantage of dolphins and porpoises. Within dolphin and porpoise herds, however, the complex social relations are less well known. At first, theories regarding order and dominance in the herd were based on observation of dolphins in captivity, limiting our knowledge to the most common captive cetacean, the bottlenose dolphin. Studies of these animals showed that males, presumably because they are generally larger than females, were the herd's leaders. Yet at sea, researchers have found that the primary bond is between mother and calf, and that some groups of dolphins and porpoises tend to travel in groups segregated by sex and age. Group partitioning, however, varies from species to species.

White and pilot whales, for example, swim in separate groups of females and calves; females, calves, and subadults; and adult groups with more males than females. Killer-whale pods, on the other hand, have a distinctive pattern of "aunting," in which females of a group help in the birth and nurturing of calves. The sperm whale's all-male "bachelor schools" are well documented: A study of a group of young male harbor porpoises at Digby Gut, in the Bay of Fundy, as well as studies of the North Atlantic bottlenose dolphin, some species of *Stenella* off Japan, and the dusky dolphin, all support the theory of separate herds for males and females, young and old.

Among the males, heavy scarring on the hides of many odontocetes testifies to their aggressive behavior when they battle for females during mating. The competition they engage in, as with most animals, is directly related to reproduction. Sperm whales, spinner and bottlenose dolphins, the dusky dolphin, and the Indo-Pacific humpbacked dolphin (among other cetaceans) compete during mating for the attention of females. Usually, this results in male members of a herd scratching other males with their teeth.

T*hough the behavior of dolphins in captivity changes markedly from their behavior in the wild, scientists can still garner much information about echolocation and other aspects of dolphin physiology in a tank like this one.*

Just as the composition of the groups is fluid, some research suggests that even leadership within herds is fluid. Christine Johnson and Ken Norris report that different individuals, regardless of age, steer the course of a group, often swimming at the rear of the herd. Johnson and Norris also say that an aggressive cetacean presents its body in a perpendicular position and will bare its teeth, snap its jaws, rapidly jerk its head or tail, and swat or ram the object or animal of its aggression. Many of these postures make the animal appear much bigger than it is—an imposing threat from anybody's perspective.

The question of a social hierarchy among dolphins makes the notion of their "cooperative" hunting something of a misnomer. Cooperation in this sense doesn't mean that the dominance within the herd changes. They simply have organized themselves to make hunting as efficient and safe as possible. Cooperation among herd members facilitates hunting: while some hunt, others protect the young. Even so, when it comes to propagating their species, males must compete for females.

C*losely related to killer whales, pilot whales also are very social animals. They sometimes gather in groups numbering a few hundred to a few thousand.*

Mating and Nurturing

In species that are monogamous, the male parent must play a role in caring for the young. Monogamy in most animal species occurs when food is scarce. Odontocetes, however, are polygynous. Most odontocete young stay with their mothers for many months, feeding on her fat-rich milk and learning to hunt. Many experts believe that the male's role in training the young is limited. Still, one male killer whale was sighted pulling an injured sea lion off the shore to allow its calf to hunt.

Males are very active participants in courtship. Chasing, leaping, and touching his potential mate with his flippers, the mating dance is a highly tactile experience. Other mating signals include tilting the body, pointing the head, and rotating and extending the flippers. Courting dolphins will also surface simultaneously and leap and beat their tails against the water. Dolphins are also famous for the "belly tilt," which is often used as a form of greeting, as a friendly pre-mating gesture, or as a bodily wave goodbye when they part. While all dolphins use these gestures at other times, they are primary mating behaviors.

In fact, Christine Johnson and Ken Norris have observed "caressing groups," in which a number of animals swim around each other, interweaving rapidly and sometimes engaging in a group belly rub. Norris and Johnson see this as a group-centered activity in which role reversal among animals takes place.

Females signal males that they are ready to mate by changes in the color of the genital area, and, in some species, the chemical composition of their urine may change, sending a signal to males in the water surrounding them. Once a male and female have swum through the courtship ritual, they finally meet, belly-to-belly, upright in the water or with the female beneath the male just below the surface. Intercourse generally lasts only a few minutes. The female must surface for air and they often must try many times before the act is complete.

Once pregnant, the females carry the fetus between ten and twelve months, though the gestation period for squid-eating species may last as long as a year and three months. Like other mammals, dolphins and porpoises bear a single, live calf. In high-

©Philip Rosenberg

latitude species births occur from spring to fall; the calving period for species living nearer the tropics isn't as seasonal. Female odontocetes giving birth often are surrounded by other females in the herd, known as "aunts." While the mother usually breaks the umbilical cord herself with a sudden twist of her body, it has been reported that a dusky dolphin in captivity came to one mother's aid and chewed through the cord. The aunts play an important role in the long life of the young with its mother. From birth, the aunts may help push the calf to the surface for its first breath of air, and, in those species that must swim faster than their young to hunt, the aunts protect the young while the mother feeds.

Young odontocetes stay with their mothers for as long as two years, nursing for a year or more, though some species do eat solid food as soon as six months after birth. (The makeup of killer-whale pods shows that females may stay with their mothers until death.) Calves swim alongside their mothers, just above her midline forward of her dorsal fin. Dolphins and porpoises may recognize each other by their distinct, and sometimes bright and colorful markings, and some research suggests that calves recognize their mothers by their whistles. A bottlenose dolphin that gave birth in captivity whistled for several days after birth, training the calf to use its acoustic receptors from the start, and perhaps teaching it to recognize her by sound. Harbor porpoises and common dolphins reach sexual maturity after three to four years, while the mammoth male killer whale will not reach maturity until sixteen years of age.

One might think that dolphins freely frolic in the ocean engaging in all kinds of touchy, sensual behavior. Nature has its own system of regulation and birth control, though, which is exemplified in the sophisticated structure of the killer whales' social units. Because they are extremely effective hunters, over-population would lead to starvation as their food supply would quickly dwindle. As members of a pod die or are captured, killer whales instinctively know that they must replace them, and the birth rate goes up.

©Pieter A. Folkens

*O*pposite page: *Though the frequency with which spotted dolphins calf isn't accurately known, researchers have observed that spotted dolphin groups affected by fishing in the Eastern Tropical Pacific mate at a younger age than normal. Left: A Risso's dolphin and calf come to the surface for air. When it is born, a Risso's dolphin is light gray. Later on it will become brown and finally attain the white and light-gray scarred hide which helps to identify this species in the wild.*

©Philip Rosenberg

A spotted dolphin calf swims alongside its mother. When it's time for the mother to feed, another female will act as an "aunt" and care for the young who are too small and slow to keep up with the rest of the herd.

The Care Givers

Odontocetes travel in large herds, stay with their young for long periods of time, and engage in touching, playful behavior just for "fun" or during mating. Observers have long pondered the epimeletic, or care-giving, behavior these cetaceans exhibit. Odontocetes have been known to stand by a fellow odontocete in distress, excitedly swim around an injured animal or charge its attacker, or actively offer support such as pushing an injured animal to the surface for air. As with their other behavioral and physiological adaptations to life in the water, these, too, have their place in nature's scheme for survival.

The social aspects of dolphin and porpoise life, coupled with their complex requirements for finding and feeding on prey, mean that calves stay with mothers to learn all these variations on life in the ocean. As humans, we engage in care-giving relationships based on our kinship relations (our progeny thrive only if we take care of them), and on reciprocity (you scratch my back, I'll scratch yours). For dolphins and porpoises, whose mother-calf bond is strong, kinship may be the primary motivator of this behavior. While some observers believe reciprocity is unlikely since dolphins' social groups are so unstable and fluid, Kenneth Norris and Christine Johnson suggest that reciprocity is at work with altruistic behavior; since the benefit of the animals' altruistic behavior is delayed, dolphins may even have some memory of their actions (see Chapter Six on memory).

Care-giving behavior springs from the strong mother-calf relationship; males rarely stand by females and never by injured males. It makes sense for females to protect and nurture their young, but in a polygynous mating system a male odontocete helping another male can only do him more harm than good in the long run. In the same way, a male standing by a female in danger risks not being able to swim away to impregnate other females. David Gaskin points out that the extra energy required for bearing and caring for air-breathing young in the water and the complexities of food gathering necessitate care-giving behavior: Other marine mammals born on land don't have to be pushed to the surface for air.

Dolphins do engage in cooperative and compassionate behavior and have a sophisticated means of communication, but can we compare them to our own? While the behaviors exist among odontocetes, their uniqueness among marine mammals perhaps heightens our interest in the "intelligence" of these mysterious creatures. It may be that dolphins and porpoises are naturally curious and "friendly" because they face no real threat from other predators and their constant search for food makes inquisitiveness about their surroundings paramount to survival.

emale killer whales—both mothers and "aunts"—are believed to be the primary caretakers and trainers of the young. However, reports from field researchers suggest that adult males often contribute to the process. One report described a male killer whale that actually pulled a sea lion off a beach, allowing its young to practice hunting.

Chapter Six

Intelligence and Communication

The human claim to fame in the evolution of all species of the animal world is their intelligence. At the top of the food chain, we are the most sophisticated of all animals. Unlike any other animals, our opposable thumbs give us the ability to make tools. The degree of coordination required for tool-making has led to the development of our large brains. We have

©Frank S. Balthis

*I*n an attempt to understand precisely how dolphins use their sounds, this researcher uses a hydrophone to listen in on the dolphins when they echolocate. One of the biggest questions facing researchers today is whether dolphins and porpoises do truly communicate with each other or simply use the sound to locate and stun their prey?

language, a sense of separateness and self, and an ability to conceptualize the future.

Recognizing that our intelligence distinguishes us from all other creatures on earth, we sometimes view other animals as too "stupid" to have any level of communciation. Dolphins and porpoises do emit sound, however, and so we try to interpret their system of "communication." We do the same with songbirds, too, but the difference is that dolphins' brains are so big that we assume, and some evidence shows, that their clicks, squeaks, and whistles indicate more than a simple instinctual call of the wild. Their highly specialized adaptation for maneuvering in the ocean, echolocation, coupled with the signals they send to each other and their friendliness and curiosity have inspired us to search for other signs of intelligent life on earth. Communicating with the animals could be viewed as one of the ways in which we strive to create, in Joseph Campbell's words, a modern myth. However, the level of communication we can achieve with dolphins is limited.

Perhaps the most well-known proponent of dolphin communication and intelligence is Dr. John C. Lilly, a psychiatrist interested in dolphin intelligence and communication, and the author of several books on the subject. During the 1960s, when Lilly predicted that humans would one day be able to communicate with dolphins, the public's response was overwhelmingly positive. Environmental issues were at the forefront of public concern, and dolphins offered a convenient and sympathetic object for public scrutiny and support. Indeed, the popularity of dolphin intelligence recalled eras past when dolphins were actually revered as mystical, powerful beings. Today, with the popularity of Gaian consciousness, shamanism, and the New Age drive to enlighten ourselves and save the earth, dolphins may once again take on nearly godlike characteristics. Focusing on dolphins' singular physiological adaptations to their environment as a means to bringing us closer to God and the androcentric dream of endowing other creatures with our own talents can be as empowering as it is dangerous: it takes dolphins out of their context—the web of nature. We know that dolphins communicate, but do their sounds imply some understanding of what they're doing or is it simply instinctual? When we say "intelligence" in regard to dolphins and porpoises, do we mean that their brains are highly developed to adapt them to their environment, or do we mean that their behavior implies that they possess mind and memory, rather than just biological reactions to environmental stimuli?

Asking how we can tell if an animal is intelligent, E.W. Menzel, Jr., of the State University of New York at Stony Brook, notes that studies of intelligence of primates, for example, has progressed from comparisons of how the subjects respond to puzzles we present to them (e.g., asking chimpanzees to fit blocks into shapes) to viewing their intelligence in terms of their response to their own environmental and social stimuli. He jokingly calls this "folk taxonomy." After all, any one of us can see when a creature is intelligent or sentient. To illustrate this, Menzel recalled a poem by Robert Frost, who, upon seeing an insect he was about to kill, sensed its fear and wrote: "I have a mind myself and recognize/Mind when I meet with it in any guise." Another manifestation of this sentiment is the push for animal rights—we somehow feel that rabbits, monkeys, dogs, and cats morally deserve better treatment. As Peter Evans succinctly put it, our response to interaction with other species "may tell us more about our own personality" than about the nature of the beast. Clearly, the question of intelligence can be answered in a number of ways: in terms of an animal's own ability to survive; by comparisons with our own behavior; philosophically, by asking if they understand what they do; or through a technological approach, asking if intelligence can be shaped or created. The ultimate answer depends on an individual's viewpoint, but where dolphins are concerned, their large brains and ability to communicate have led scientists to some fascinating research.

BRAINS

The study of dolphin communication and intelligence is little more than 100 years old, and only in the last twenty or thirty years, as the public's interest was sparked and research funds became available, has it become a popular issue. In fact, the study of the differences between human and animal biology didn't begin until the sixteenth century with the work of the Italian anatomist Andreas Vesalius. Later, once the relationship between the brain and our bodily functions and perceptions was recognized, the size and complexity of our brains distinguished us from all other animals. During the peak whaling years, between the eighteenth and nineteenth centuries, scientists had the opportunity to study the brains of cetaceans. According to John Lilly, early research on intelligence concentrated on comparisons between the size of the cetacean brain and the similarity of their cerebral cortex with ours, almost wholly ignoring the behavior of the animal. Even though brains of larger whales were big and dolphin and porpoise brains were shown to be large in proportion to their bodies, the prevailing attitude was that whales and dolphins had to have large brains to maintain their large bodies. A comparison like this ignores the fact that

This researcher (below) *is using a recording device to listen to the echolocation sounds emitted by dolphins. In studying echolocation, scientists hope to gain a greater knowledge of dolphin and porpoise intelligence and communication.*

©Frank S. Balthis

©Randy Wells

many large animals, notably the dinosaurs, had small brains in proportion to their body size. The messages that needed to be sent by the dinosaur body, however, were not as complex as the messages that humans or dolphins need to send. Pieter Folkens likens this to comparing the operating systems, or DOS, of Apple and IBM computers. The DOS required to run these systems serve the same function, but neither can speak to the other—their coding is entirely different. Likewise, the system that drives cetaceans and the system that drives humans are quite different.

While some early observers of dolphins and porpoises recognized their friendliness and ability to communicate, it wasn't until behavioral studies of dolphins and porpoises in the early 1960s that our fascination with the dolphin brain led to serious discussion of their intelligence. Researchers still rely on the study of the brain alone, pointing out that the cerebral cortex of dolphins and porpoises is similar to humans' and that the neo-

cortex, which controls the parts of our brains that create and reason, covers more of the dolphin's cortex than our own. The portion of the dolphin's cortex that controls its acoustic abilities is as large as our own visual cortex, though acoustic information may be more difficult to store and retrieve than visual information. Yet the "encephalisation quotient" (EQ), which measures the ratio of an animal's brain surface area to its body surface area, provides a more accurate standard for measuring intelligence. The higher the EQ, the more surface area in an animal's brain. Just as the wire for speakers has more surface area than a single wire (speaker wire being made of several separate wires twisted together) in order to conduct electricity with definition, a brain with a high EQ can conduct more messages. With the human EQ at about 7.4 and the chimpanzee's at 2.5, an argument for high dolphin intelligence can be made considering the bottlenose dolphin's EQ of 5.6, with the porpoise EQ being slightly lower.

©Randy Wells

U*sing sophisticated equipment, (opposite page), researchers at the University of California at Santa Cruz record the vocalizations of a bottlenose dolphin.*

L*eft: Researchers at the University of California at Santa Cruz record the sounds of a mother bottlenose dolphin and her calf to learn when and why dolphins make certain sounds.*

COMMUNICATION AND THE 'MIND'

We need to know more about an animal than simply the structure and size of its brain before we can begin to define its intelligence. Today's research also relies on the behavior of dolphins and porpoises to define intelligence. Ken Norris and his colleague Christine Johnson at the Center for Marine Studies in Santa Cruz believe that "the essentially communal and behaviorally variable dolphins may have been selected to develop certain complex cognitive abilities." Their studies of dolphin communication and behavior have led them to the conclusion that dolphins' cognitive abilities are necessary ingredients for survival: without them, they could not hunt in groups. Likewise, the ground-breaking work of Louis Herman, in which dolphins have learned some elements of language, also suggests a unique dolphin intelligence. Yet David Gaskin warns that while dolphins are indeed good mimics and have excellent auditory skills, these abilities do not necessarily equal intelligence. Illustrating his point, Gaskin relates that even though his cat has learned to open doors, he can't assume the cat consciously has a plan, purpose, or intent: "*Purpose* and *intent* imply some foreknowledge of the specific results of specific actions. The more definitive studies on dolphin behaviour suggest (despite statements to the contrary) that dolphins have not yet been demonstrated to have thought processes of this kind."

Yet dolphins at Marine World/Africa USA would refute Gaskin's argument. A group of dolphins were taught to pick up the trash in their pool and bring it to a trainer for a fish reward, and one dolphin seemed to find more trash than any of the others. The dolphin's trainer, Jim Mullen, discovered that it had hidden several bags under a platform. The dolphin would tear off a piece and take it to the trainer for his reward, then return to the bag to tear off another piece and score yet another fish. The dolphin exploited this reward system without any training. It definitely had a purpose and intent when it hid the trash.

Dolphins' free time in captivity is one of the factors leading to their increased creativity and intelligence. At sea they must concentrate on hunting and surviving; in a pool they have time to devise games for themselves, like duping their trainer into giving them extra bits of fish. Killer whales, too, seek to amuse themselves in captivity. Some will bite off the fins of the fish they're being fed and surround them with bubbles. The killer whales seem to watch with fascination as light plays off the bubble-encased fins as they float to the surface.

K*iller whales aren't the only species of ondontocete that allow themselves to be viewed as readily as this. It's little wonder, then, that we humans have allowed our innate curiosity to wander to the philosophical and biological questions of dolphin communication.*

A researcher at the University of California at Santa Cruz trains Jo, a bottlenose dolphin, in order to conduct experiments that will reveal more about the dolphin's ability to communicate.

In this photograph (right), *Dr. Louis Herman works with Akeakamai. Herman and his colleagues at the Kewalo Basin Marine Mammal Laboratory in Honolulu, Hawaii, have succeeded in creating a basic vocabulary for Akeakamai and the other dolphins with which they work.*

©Randy Wells

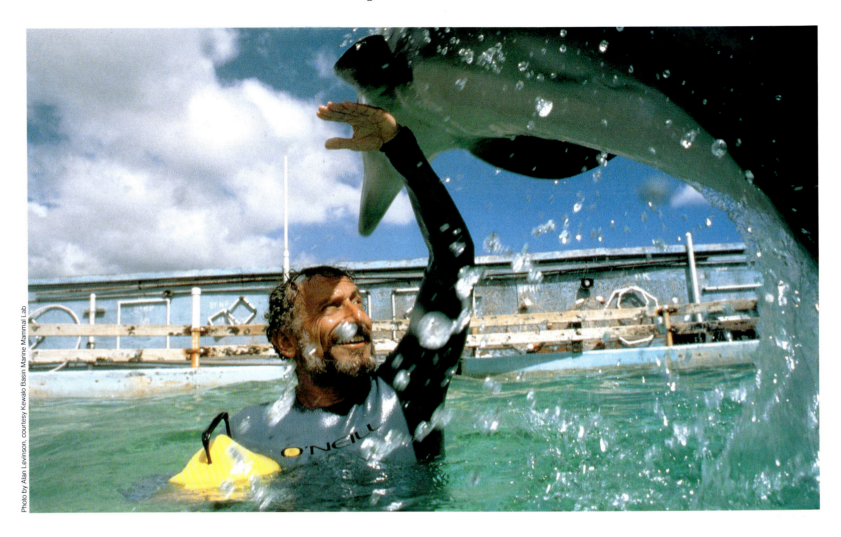

Photo by Alan Levinson, courtesy Kewalo Basin Marine Mammal Lab

The work of Louis Herman signifies a remarkable departure from the popular studies of communication with dolphins and chimpanzees conducted during the 1960s. Herman argues that in trying to teach apes language the emphasis was on getting the animals to produce language, not to understand it. Also, the studies with apes were marred by inefficient controls: some of the results show that the apes constructed sentences because of prompts from the trainers. While John Lilly's experiments with dolphins showed their capacity to mimic sounds, Louis Herman's work has taken dolphins' ability to mimic sounds one step farther. Using both sounds and gestures, Herman and his colleagues have succeeded in getting dolphins not only to label, or "name," objects but to perform actions based on simple sentence structure. He created both a basic vocabulary and syntactic rules for using language and tested it on two bottlenose dolphins named Phoenix and Akeakamai. For example, after the dolphin has learned to label an object with its name, the auditory command "FRISBEE FETCH HOOP" tells the dolphin to take the Frisbee to the hoop and stay there. This same command can be expressed in a different sequence, using a gestural command: HOOP FRISBEE FETCH. In the first command, the relation of the words and actions is linear; in the second, gestural command, the sentence is constructed in inverse language. "The grammatical function of the first object word cannot be assigned until the second word appears.... Instead, the response to the first word in the sequence must be reserved until the grammatical function of that word as direct or indirect object is resolved by the succeeding word." Using this created language, Herman successfully showed that the grammar need not be linear to be utilized by the dolphin. In addition, Herman tested the dolphins' visual responses and found that the dolphins did not respond as well until an auditory name was assigned. Even so, showing that the dolphin could use both its vision and hearing to complete the tests showed a high degree of good generalized cognitive skills.

In its early days, dolphin research often went hand-in-hand with training dolphins for performances in marine-park shows. Below: *A visitor touches the mouth of a bottlenose dolphin at Marine World in Vallejo, California.*

©Frank S. Balthis

©James D. Watt

Spectacular acrobats in the wild, dolphins' natural habits seem extraordinary in captivity. Above: *At Sea Life Park in Hawaii a bottlenose dolphin jumps for its reward of fish.*

To complete these tests, the dolphins utilized their auditory short-term memory, actually building a vocabulary of symbols and sentences. While no one has yet found conclusive proof of dolphins' own natural language, Herman's tests show that dolphins are capable of at least learning a language. He suggests that while the skills tested may not be used in the wild they do show a relationship between the dolphins' social behavior—both their tendency to travel in groups and their epimeletic behavior (see page 92)—and their cognitive abilities. Dolphin young take a long time to mature, and extensive care-giving is necessary, suggesting that the concept of altruism (see page 92) may exist among them. As we saw in Chapter Five, the response time of altruism is delayed, because the care giver does not receive any reward immediately, which means that the dolphin must have some capacity for memory. As Ken Norris puts it, reciprocal altruism "requires that its members be fairly long-lived, experience a relatively extensive period of development in which they may learn appropriate responses in a variety of social contexts, and have memories adequate to the task of keeping track of other individuals and the status of their relationships. Dolphins apparently meet all of these requirements."

THE INTELLIGENCE CONTINUUM

John Lilly proposed that dolphins made sounds to elicit a particular response from other members of their species; others disagreed, saying that the sounds were only signals offering information about a group's location and environment. The latest work by Louis Herman suggests only that dolphins have the capability of memory and of learning language—his results cannot be interpreted to mean that dolphins actually communicate with each other. Do dolphins understand the consequences of their behavior? Do they actually communicate with each other or are they just sending signals? We may never understand the dolphins' own system of codes used in their natural habitat, but whether following strictly Darwinian precepts of selection and evolution or a heuristic approach combining bits of philosophy and anthropomorphism with science, dolphins' capabilities surely can't be taken lightly. Their performances at the lab and at marine-park shows may be supremely entertaining, but their potential and training may involve them in human endeavors nearly too fantastic to imagine.

Chapter Seven

In Training

t marine park shows, dolphins and porpoises appear to flash a knowing and friendly smile at the audience as they perform their daredevil acrobatics, leaping and twisting and spinning. Our perceptions can be deceiving: like the penguin's "suit," the dolphin's "smile" is merely the result of biology—the shape of its head and jaw.

While not beyond the leaps and spins they perform naturally in the wild, their stunts are designed to please the crowd. Entertaining human fancies of a wild animal trained just for us, dolphins, like horses and dogs, are slowly being domesticated. In captivity, their behavior slowly changes, until they finally lose their instincts for survival in the wild. Their talents—miming and performing tricks—show researchers their cognitive abilities, while the military capitalizes on them for underwater reconnaissance. Still others look to dolphins for help with farming our oceans. Jacques Cousteau termed dolphins' involvement in experiments like these a "collaboration." While it's true that dolphins in captivity rarely, if ever, try to escape, the dolphins' efforts are not some instinctive desire to please—rather, we mold them to our own needs and amusement. At a marine-park show, the ultimate goal is sheer fun.

Many captive dolphins are third-, fourth-, or fifth-generation descendants of ancestors who lived in the wild. Though dolphin trainers and researchers have made tremendous strides in understanding and manipulating dolphin behavior, it took 10,000 years of crossbreeding to domesticate animals such as horses, dogs, and cats. Dolphins and porpoises clearly have a long way to go.

I*n California at San Diego's Sea World* (below) *and Vallejo's Marine World* (left) *killer whales perform both simultaneous and singular leaps to please the crowd.*

©Frank S. Balthis

Though known to humans at least since recorded history, it wasn't until the early twentieth century that dolphins were successfully kept in captivity. This illustration demonstrates just how far dolphin research and medicine has come. Dr. Frank Buckland was charged with the care of porpoises at the Zoological Gardens in London in 1863. Among the cures he prescribed for their care were brandy and water. Not surprisingly, only one of the three porpoises lived—and that one only for a short time.

CAPTURE AND TRANSPORT

Dolphins were first captured for display in captivity in Europe during the mid-nineteenth century, though these early attempts at stocking aquariums with dolphins were unsuccessful. One dolphin caught in 1862 for the London Zoo lived only one day. After repeated attempts, in 1913 the New York Aquarium succeeded in keeping the first dolphin in captivity alive. Today, in addition to the ubiquitous bottlenose dolphin, oceanariums and marine-park shows entertain their audiences with Pacific white-sided dolphins, belugas, pilot whales, and, relative newcomers because they are the most difficult to catch—but instant hits—killer whales.

Marine parks and oceanariums as we know them are less than sixty years old. The first, Marine Studios (now Marineland of Florida), in St. Augustine, Florida, opened in 1938, the first to keep a breeding colony of bottlenose dolphins. Though examples of friendly dolphins are many, capturing them without injury and helping them to adapt and survive in captivity took years of trial and error and the unfortunate loss of many dolphins and porpoises.

Even though the dolphin, a top predator in the sea, doesn't yet recognize humans as predators (in fact, a group of porpoises washed out of their home at Marineland of Florida by a hurricane returned to the site to watch as workers reconstructed their tank, and some species willingly swim near ships and people), capturing any delphinid species was initially no easy task. Before dolphin observers knew about echolocation, the animal's ability to elude would-be captors' nets was maddening.

In his account of the early study of dolphins, *The Porpoise Watcher*, Ken Norris tells the frustrating story of trying to cap-

ture dolphins and porpoises for Marineland of the Pacific in Los Angeles, the world's second oceanarium. When the oceanarium opened, in 1954, it had only three bottlenose dolphins, which it had borrowed from Marineland of Florida. As the park's curator, Norris was determined to capture his own dolphins. Florida's Marineland had the distinct advantage of waterways behind it in which dolphins swam. While scores of common dolphins playfully rode off the bow of Norris's boat, and Dall's porpoises were sighted, catching them proved time-consuming and frustrating. Little was known of their ability to echolocate, something Arthur McBride, the first curator of Florida's Marineland, learned the hard way when he tried to catch them with nets.

Guessing that the dolphins made sounds that they somehow bounced off his nets, McBride finally captured them by making the mesh of the nets larger. When Norris tried to capture porpoises by encircling them in a net, they escaped before he could completely close it. He finally outsmarted them by placing a net parallel to the shore and far enough out so they would swim into it, unable to detect it with their sonar. Once inside, the fishermen pulled the ends shut, trapping the dolphins inside.

Today's methods for catching dolphins and porpoises, though slightly more sophisticated, differ little from these early methods. To catch deep-water species, a net is placed over the dolphin's head as it rides the bow waves of the boat. Once the net is in place, a diver joins the dolphin in the water and places it in a sling to be hoisted aboard the ship. Dolphins who live closer to land are driven toward shore, where they are caught in nets, much as Norris and his colleagues first discovered. While making the trip to shore, the dolphin is kept moist with towels and

T hree spinner dolphins (below), *though in danger of becoming the victims of tuna purse-seine fishing, swim freely in their ocean habitat.*

©James D. Watt

repeated doses of cold water, and kept out of the sun to avoid injuring its sensitive hide. When it is moved from the boat to the tank, handlers take care to avoid grasping its flippers or flukes, which can too easily be hurt if handled improperly.

In captivity, dolphins must make many adjustments to their new habitat. In addition to the dangers of disease and lung infection (as a result of increased pressure on the lungs during transport time out of the water), the behavior of dolphins changes radically in captivity. They must learn to eat dead or frozen fish, and a dolphin that is dominant in the wild may not have the same leadership role in the tank, because all the dolphins are hand-fed. In his book, Ken Norris describes the behavioral changes that occur in dolphins:

> In captivity usually two or more species are thrown together into unnatural assemblages that seldom or never exist in nature. Confinement compresses a porpoise's activity, no matter how large the tank. The difference is between forty to sixty miles of daily travel and movement in a tank two hundred feet in diameter. The difference is the chance to dive out of sight of the surface—perhaps to over a thousand feet for some porpoises—versus perhaps twenty-five feet in captivity. The difference is a limitless world where aggression and fear can reorder social structure within and between schools and a world where these forces are contained by cement walls. In captivity shy porpoises can't move far away from aggressive ones. In fact, confinement compresses natural activity so tightly that it may be distorted virtually beyond recognition. The captive porpoise forms unnatural life patterns, like the antelope in the zoo, used to ranging many miles a day, who comes to promenade in a stereotyped figure eight around his cage until the single track is rutted a foot below the surrounding soil.

Clearly, the transition from life in the open sea to life in a tank is a stressful one. To make the dolphins' stay as comfortable and healthy as possible, they are fed a variety of fish and manufactured food (very much like dog or cat food), which is supplemented with vitamins. The water in the tank, usually manufactured salt water, is carefully monitored for its pH level, temperature, salinity, and cleanliness. Fungi and bacteria in the water develop quickly if copper and chlorine are not added.

Dolphins do adjust to life in the tank, however. Though some get "depressed" and refuse to show off their talents, most acclimate to their new environs. While purists might argue that taking an animal out of its habitat and forcing it to dramatically change its behavior is immoral, dolphins in marine parks help bring the plight of their cousins in the wild to the public's atten-

O*n the TV show "Flipper," the dolphin called to his friends Buddy and Sandy and made this winning "smile" (above) famous.*

tion. Killer whales, once so despised that a Monterey, California, newspaper headline warned "Watch Out Ladies, There's a Killer on the Loose," have since taken their rightful place as creatures to be respected and protected. Mamu, the first killer whale to survive in captivity, at the Vancouver Public Aquarium, was instrumental in changing the public's attitude about cetaceans. When they are able to watch dolphins exhibit their intelligence and playfulness, people more readily respond to conservationists' cries for the protection of these animals.

Dolphins' new training regimen for the playful capture of balls and leaping through hoops isn't all fun and games, however. In fact, the science of tricks isn't far removed from the science of their behavior. Ken Norris's own research on echolocation and

dolphin behavior began with a dolphin named Kathy, who was loaned to him by a marine-park for research, on the condition that he teach her a new repertoire of games to entertain her audiences. Norris and his assistant John Prescott learned how to blindfold Kathy—not an easy task on the slippery cetacean's hide—and discovered that she could swim to objects in the water blind. These experiments, performed for a television show about dolphin communication, provided publicity for Marineland of the Pacific, where the experiments took place; added pizzazz to the show; and offered new tricks for her audience at Marine Studios (now Marineland of Florida) where she lived. According to Norris, most early experiments with captive dolphins were carried out on dolphins owned by marine parks.

R*ight: A bottlenose dolphin leaps through a train-er's hoop in Fort Lauderdale, Florida. Opposite page: Killer whales perform simultaneous leaps at marine-park shows.*

AT PLAY: Dolphins in Marine Park Shows

Whether dolphins and porpoises inhabit a tank just to be admired by observers or for their tricks, their popularity among all captive marine mammals is unsurpassed. From the Long Marine Lab's "touch tanks," where 30,000 visitors a year get first-hand contact with the animals, to Epcot Center's Living Seas exhibit, which includes the world's largest aquarium—some six million gallons of manufactured seawater—and attracts some twenty-two million visitors a year, dolphins and porpoises inevitably steal the show. All over the world, marine parks and aquariums provide a popular tourist attraction: at Great Britain's Flamingo Park (Malton, Yorkshire) and Whipsnade Zoological Gardens (Bedfordshire); at Canada's Vancouver Public Aquarium and Niagara Falls exhibit; in Queensland, Australia; and in Holland, Belgium, France, and Spain. (See the Sources section at the end of this book for a complete list of aquariums and marine parks.)

At the parks, dolphins and porpoises perform tricks that stagger the imagination. Performing spectacular triple somersaults, leaping through hoops, and fetching balls, Frisbees, and all manner of other toys, some animals actually execute stunts that go against the grain of their natural survival instincts. One performance features a dolphin or killer whale rising vertically out of the water to "kiss" its trainer, standing at the edge of the pool, while other dolphins strand themselves on the side of the tank. Synchronized leaps, skimming vertically across the water on their tails, and all the other tricks that dolphins perform, while appearing to be just good fun, aren't performed without some reward from the trainers.

Teaching dolphins and porpoises to perform their marine-park antics takes weeks of conditioning, in which the dolphins are given a reward of tasty fish for successfully completing a task. At first, trainers relied on operant conditioning, in which a

H*ere,* (right) *bottlenose dolphins tail-walk much to the delight of marine-park audiences. Though this isn't one of their more common behaviors in the wild, it is a sure crowd pleaser.*

C*ontrary to its aggressive hunting behavior in the wild, a killer whale kisses its trainer* (opposite page) *for a fish reward.*

reward (fish) is meted out for successfully completed tasks and a punishment (an electric shock) for a wrong move; observers discovered, however, that the punishment did more to hinder the animal's performance than help it.

Trainers know that dolphins are social animals and that the bond between a female and her calf is the strongest of all bonds (see page 92). Capitalizing on this natural bond, trainers can often get young dolphins to mimic the trainer's gestures, as if the trainer were "mother." Likewise, in a group of dolphins in captivity, a lead female plays an important role in leading the dolphins in their performance and is often the one with whom the other dolphins perform their simultaneous leaps. Eventually the animals learn to perform their tasks without reward, but by starting small and building up to more complicated tricks the trainer gives rewards along the way. Training may begin with something as simple as getting the dolphin to swim through a hoop or to retrieve a ball or toy on command. Once these relatively simple tasks are learned, the animals graduate to a complicated series of commands, which the work of Louis Herman may one day increase.

©Birgit Winning/EarthViews

AT WORK: Dolphins and Reconnaissance

Just as there is a symbiotic relationship between dolphins' training for play and researchers' needs, the talents of dolphins and porpoises are also recognized in more practical spheres of life. The United States Navy has demonstrated an interest in dolphins' talents since they were first brought to light during the early 1960s. In addition to training dolphins to complete tasks with and for divers in the water, the Navy learned a lesson in hydrodynamics from the dolphins' superior swimming profile. The shape of our modern nuclear submarines was inspired by the dolphin's streamlined body.

The Naval Undersea Research and Development Center at San Diego, California, and the Oceanographic Institute of Hawaii at Honolulu, the primary research centers for the study of dolphins, succeeded in training dolphins not only to respond to their trainers in enclosed tank conditions but also to work with them at sea. For military purposes, dolphins and sea lions have been trained to help divers, bringing them tools when they work underwater. In Vietnam, dolphins were trained to take a dart filled with carbon dioxide and puncture an enemy diver, causing him to explode. The United States Navy, recognizing the value of dolphins' ability to echolocate, has experimented with placing a metal plate on the side of its submarines. When dolphins are instructed to place mines on enemy vessels, they avoid American submarines because they can "see" the metal plate. (see page 84 on echolocation).

One bottlenose dolphin named Tuffy was even taught to respond to the call of a diver in distress. Working on the sea floor in *Sealabs II* and *III*, divers carried electric bells to call Tuffy should they become disoriented and need to be led back to the station. At the sound of the bell, Tuffy would take a rope from the sea station to the diver, who could then find his way to the base.

Like Tuffy, Ken Norris's dolphin Keiki was first trained in an enclosed area; when Keiki was asked to make the transition to open water, she at first resisted. And, like Tuffy, Keiki was used for a study of an undersea lab, where she was asked to carry things from the surface to the divers. She also allowed the divers to hold onto her dorsal fin so they could be towed to the surface. As in the tank, at first the researchers rewarded Keiki with fish after each successful task. Using fish in shark-infested waters, however, proved dangerous to the divers, and plastic tokens were substituted, which Keiki could later trade in for fish.

These experiments point to the important role dolphins

©Pieter A. Folkens

could play in our search for new food sources. In aquaculture, for example, dolphins and porpoises might be trained to swim along fences surrounding underwater farms detecting poachers. Or they could aid farmers by carrying samples and tools to and from workers. Unfortunately, these potential benefits are only theoretical. Research on aquaculture, once slow at best, due to lack of funds, is now virtually nonexistent, and the level of toxins and wastes in our oceans threaten to limit even that once bountiful resource.

Even so, as researchers learn more about dolphins' potential to learn new tricks, and as those tricks come to be known to the public, dolphins and porpoises surely will continue to ride a high tide. Dolphins' overwhelming popularity at marine-park shows and aquariums attests to the public's affection for them, and fuels its concern for the future of these talented and friendly creatures of the sea.

S*wimming with a pod of pilot whales* (opposite page),

divers use sophisticated underwater photographic equipment

to record their movements. Above: *Weekend yachting enthu-*

siasts delight in being accompanied by killer whales.

Chapter Eight

A Peaceful Coexistence?

S ince the 1970s, the drive to "save the whales" has waned and gained momentum in fits and starts. Some see the whales as icons of the animal-rights movement while others hope that the popularity of whale-saving will lead humans away from their homocentricity. The dolphin's cognitive ability, its reputation as a friend to humans, and its incredible echolocation

©Marc Webber

S triped dolphins, members of the same genus as the

spotted and spinner dolphins (stenella) *that fishing boats use*

to find yellowfin tuna, travel in much the same way their

cousins do. When fishers spot the dolphins, they can be sure

tuna are nearby and trap both in their nets.

abilities all make it a creature for which humans feel sympathy. Whatever the motivations or implications of wanting to save dolphins, porpoises, and whales from their certain danger in today's oceans, the fact remains that many species of dolphins and porpoises are endangered and severely depleted.

While the most popular topics of debate presently regarding dolphin mortality are their mysterious deaths from disease in the Baltic Sea and off the Eastern Coast of the United States and the effect the tuna fishing industry has on dolphin populations, many other factors are at work to endanger the animals. Bacteria and waste in the oceans, dolphin hunting by native populations, and the incidental (or accidental) kill of dolphins by boats, while they may not seem serious taken individually, do have far-reaching ramifications when considered as a whole.

DOLPHINS AND TUNA

Tuna boats follow spinner, spotted, and white-bellied common dolphins to find their yellowfin tuna catch in the Eastern Tropical Pacific (ETP), an area of the Pacific Ocean from Southern California to Chile. The spinner dolphin population in this area seems to be sensitive to the tuna schools. While observers once thought that tuna swam beneath and a little ways behind herds of spinners, more recent studies show that the dolphins may also follow the tuna. With humans fishing the seas, however, their symbiotic relationship with tuna puts the dolphins in danger. Before 1960, the tuna boats would throw bait into the water, throwing the tuna into a feeding "frenzy." The fishermen would then cast hooks into the water—the dolphins wouldn't bite because of their sophisticated sonar, but the tuna would. With the introduction of purse-seine fishing after 1960, the dolphins were put at serious risk. The purse-seine, a large net that encircles the dolphins and the tuna and traps them when the net is pulled shut at the bottom, has killed an estimated seven and a half million dolphins since its widespread use by commercial fishing boats began. Despite efforts by environmentalists and conservationists, which led to the passage of the Marine Mammal Protection Act of 1972, purse-seine fishing of tuna, endangering the dolphin population, continues in the ETP.

Before 1981, fewer than half of the tuna caught in this region were captured using nets. Since then, bait fishing for tuna has all but disappeared. Large commercial vessels, which can accommodate large numbers of tuna as well bear the costs, have all but eradicated the small, bait-fishing boat. While commercial fishermen argue that killing the dolphins is "incidental," conservationists counter that the dolphins are purposely chased and encircled. In addition, no one knows how many of the thousands of dolphins that escape the nets swim off to die of injuries, such as torn flippers and flukes, incurred while in the net. Most disruptive of all to the dolphin population is the high percentage of pregnant animals and their calves that are injured. In 1986, over 80 percent of the dolphins killed as a result of tuna fishing were pregnant females.

The passage of the Marine Mammal Protection Act of 1972 (MMPA) was a first step in saving the dolphin population. It called for a quota on the number of dolphins killed each year (with the aim of eventually reducing the kill to nothing), and required that U.S. tuna-fishing boats allow observers on board to report any infractions and to count kills. In addition, the MMPA instituted research into dolphin-saving techniques: refining the Medina panel, a net with smaller mesh so that dolphin flippers and beaks won't get caught as easily, and the "back-down" procedure. While the MMPA was successful in establishing quotas, the

National Marine Fisheries Service (NMFS) has had difficulty policing their rulings. The Inter-American Tropical Tuna Commission (IATTC), originally formed in 1950 between Costa Rica and the U.S., is responsible for studying the biology of tuna and recommending ways to maintain the population of tuna in the oceans. Though the NMFS and the IATTC both observe fishing practices firsthand on tuna boats, the IATTC observers do not report violations. Compounding the problem, between 1981 and 1984 tuna boats were not required to allow NMFS observers aboard, and until 1988 women were not allowed as observers because fishermen said they would "destroy morale" on board the ship. Though NMFS observers, men and women alike, now must be allowed aboard U.S. ships, the size of the U.S. fleet has shrunk while the foreign fleet has grown, and the powerful economic and political lobby of the tuna industry has resulted in relaxing of regulations.

Complaining that their tuna catch has fallen, commercial fishermen lobbied for and won an indefinite extension of the dolphin-kill quota of 20,500 in 1984. Those who argue that the

©Marine Mammal Fund

©Marine Mammal Fund

T he photographs on the next four pages were clandestinely taken by an observer on a fishing boat practicing purse-seine fishing. Left: *a fisherman stoops over a fishing net to remove a trapped dolphin.* Above: *Dolphins are caught in tuna nets.* Next page: *A Dall's porpoise caught in a net has little chance for survival if its delicate flippers and dorsal fin are damaged. If being trapped in the fishing net isn't bad enough, when the net is pulled aboard the ship, sometimes the dolphin trapped in it is mangled by the block and tackle.*

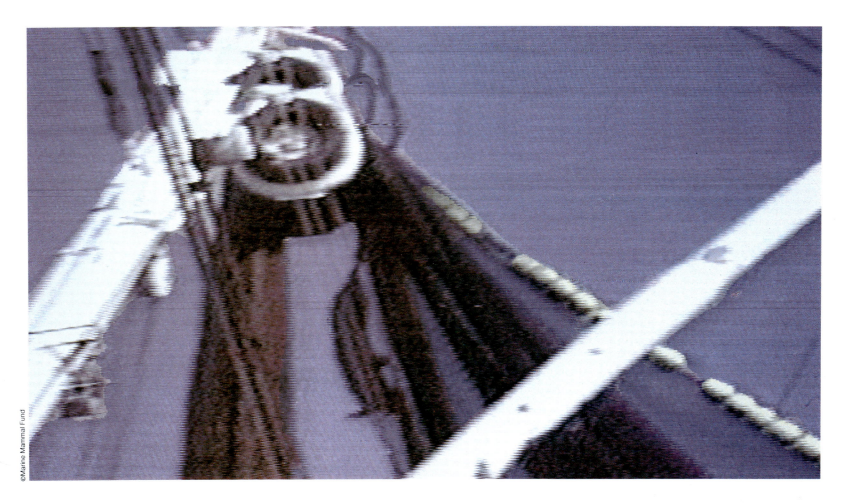

©Marine Mammal Fund

quota should continue to go down, as was specified in the original MMPA, say that the tuna industry has brought about its own demise. Between 1967 and 1985, the amount of tuna available from fishermen skyrocketed, which brought the price down. In addition, the U.S. fleet, once the most productive in the world, is now half the size of all foreign fleets combined. During the 1980s, other regulations, such as a moratorium on nighttime fishing, were relaxed. According to an IATTC report, night hauls of tuna kill four times as many dolphins as daytime catches. And research into dolphin-saving techniques has virtually disappeared due to lack of research funds available during the Reagan Administration.

As the battle continues to rage between conservationists and government and industry forces, the impact of the foreign fleet is a pressing concern. The reported 125,000 dolphins killed by foreign fishermen far exceeds the United States quota of 20,500, and unofficial estimates of the kills are twice as high. No international organization controls or polices the catch or methods of foreign fishermen. Yet the tuna bought from these foreign fleets does make it into the U.S. consumer market. Consumer groups are pressuring the two major tuna-buying corporations, Ralston Purina (Chicken of the Sea) and H.J. Heinz (Starkist Tuna), to stop buying tuna that has involved injury to dolphins.

Only 5 percent of worldwide tuna-fishing involves dolphin kills. While the majority of tuna fishing outside the ETP does dolphins no harm, the effect of unchecked purse-seine fishing surely will have consequences on the tuna industry itself as well as on the already fragile dolphin population. The Earth Island Institute and the Marine Mammal Fund filed a lawsuit in 1988 demanding that the Commerce Department stop issuing permits to tuna importers who don't follow MMPA guidelines for dolphin-saving techniques and still use purse-seine fishing; the litigation also charges that the United States has not developed and instituted methods to lower dolphin kills as stipulated in the MMPA.

As conservationists and environmentalists continue to struggle with the power of big business, dolphins and porpoises roam seas that, for these and many other reasons, become increasingly hostile to them.

T*his Japanese poster* (above) *is an advertisement for whale meat. The Japanese have been notoriously negligent in developing laws that prohibit or limit the killing of whales and dolphins for food.*

T*his spectacular photograph from Greenpeace* (opposite page) *shows how spotted dolphins are needlessly trapped in fishing nets, leading to the senseless deaths of thousands of dolphins per year.*

DANGER FOR OTHER DOLPHINS

While the battle to save dolphins trapped in tuna nets has captured the public's attention, dangers to other species of dolphins and porpoises have received less press time. The Amazon River dolphin, or Amazon pink, faces extinction due to human interference in its habitat. Once a plentiful river-dolphin species that was revered by Brazilians as a magical, mystical creature, they're now hunted by fishermen, who sell their dried sex organs and eyeballs as good-luck pieces. Dams built by agribusinesses pose the biggest threat to these dolphins; in 1985, two hundred of them were killed behind a dam some 500 miles north of Brasilia.

The Cochito, called Vaquita by Mexican fishermen, in the Gulf of California are also threatened with extinction. Discovered in the 1950s by Ken Norris, the rare Vaquita emits a high-pitched sound unlike any other known dolphin or porpoise. Though killing marine mammals was outlawed in Mexico, researchers fear that this endangered species may not recover, noting that commercial fishermen have officially reported only ten sightings of the animal and they themselves reported only about 100. All over the world, dolphins and porpoises fall prey to wanton and careless fishing and hunting practices. Not realizing that the oceans' bounty is limited, countries from Turkey to Chile to Japan continue to hunt even those species proved to be endangered or depleted.

Hunted for their meat and oil, dolphins also meet their demise from Turkish and Japanese fishermen who believe that dolphins threaten their own catch of fish. While the Soviet Union, Bulgaria, and Rumania stopped hunting common and bottlenose dolphins in the Black Sea after the dolphin population dropped drastically between 1964 and 1966, Turkey continues to allow anyone to shoot dolphins in open season (between October 1st and May 19th). Though the Council of Europe's Convention on

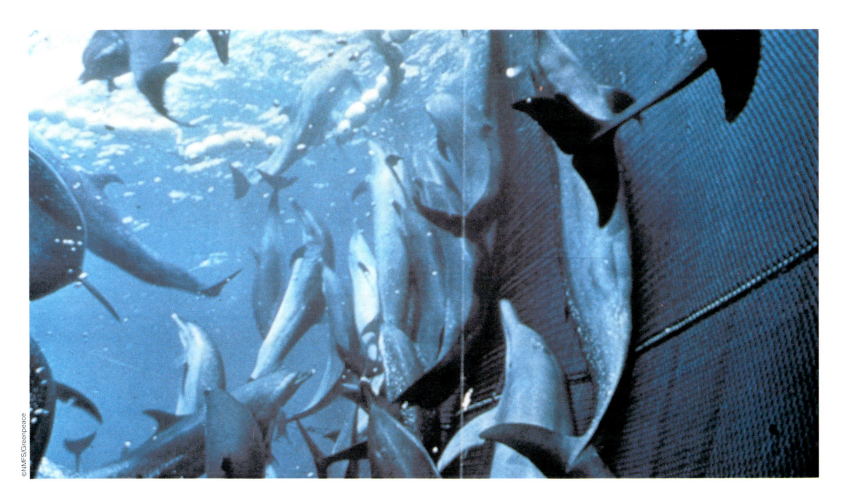

©NMFS/Greenpeace

the Conservation of European Wildlife and Natural Habitats rati-
fied a treaty in 1981 protecting bottlenose and common dolphins
and harbor porpoises, Turkey refused to cooperate. Even though
the dolphin population continues to drop, and Turkey's market
for the animals has been reduced since the 1981 ban on imported
whale products by the European Economic Community, pleas
from environmentalists have fallen on deaf ears.

The list of senseless dolphin kills goes on. In Chile, fishermen
use dolphin meat as bait for southern king crabs, killing some
10,000 dolphins and Burmeister's porpoises a year. Japanese
fishermen, too, are responsible for reducing the spinner dolphin
population in the Gulf of Alaska, and for reducing the Dall's porpoise population to an estimated half of its original size. Around
the islands of Japan, fishermen kill dolphins under the mistaken
assumption that they pose a threat to their own take. In Iceland,
the seemingly worthwhile venture of capturing killer whales for
sale to research facilities and marine parks in Europe (the United
States outlawed purchase of these animals in 1981) has taken its
toll on at least five orca lives. The whaler *Gudrun* catches the
killers and delivers them to the Saedyrasanfned Aquarium,
where they are exported to other countries. While the number
of dolphins affected by this practice is quite small, the disregard
the aquarium has shown for the safe and healthy transport and
care of the killers once they arrive has outraged environmentalists. In 1981, one of three killers sold to the Clacton Pier
Seaquarium in the United Kingdom died as a result of being hit
by his two tank-mates. The workers at the aquarium thought the
orcas' behavior was simply playful.

D*rift-net fishing poses an even more serious*

threat to marine life than does purse-seine fishing of tuna.

Drift nets spread over several miles, trapping everything

within their forty foot depth.

T his oil spill off the coast of Brittany, France occurred in the spring of 1978. Spills like this one are endangering the entire dolphin and porpoise population.

INSIDIOUS WASTE, INSIDIOUS DEATH: Pollutants and Disease

By far the most insidious threat to dolphins and porpoises is the one that will have the most direct effect on our own lives: pollution and toxic wastes in our waters. Concern about the effect of pollution on our planet's once bountiful resources reached the public with the publication of Rachel Carson's *Silent Spring* and the subsequent ecology movement of the late 1960s and early 1970s. Though the harmful effects of pollutants in our air, earth, and sea have been studied and tested for decades, we continue to dump waste into our oceans with a dump-it-now, test-the-effects-later attitude. Though dolphins, like other mammals, are subject to natural diseases of their own, they, like humans, are suffering the effects of disease as a result of the toxins and wastes humans dump into the ocean either directly or indirectly.

Environmentalists have long been concerned with the dumping of pollutants in our waters. The trend of beach closings during the latter part of the 1980s on the Northeastern coast of the United States has finally brought the public's attention to this problem. While pollution destroys many people's summer fun— what good is a beach if you can't swim there?—pollutants such as DDT (and its derivatives, aldrin and dieldrin) and PCB (polychlorinated biphenyl) affect the production of plankton, the basis of life in the sea. Plankton, composed of phytoplankton and zooplankton, is the first link in the ocean's food chain. Krill and fish, the staples in many marine mammals' diets, feed on plankton, and we in turn feed on the fish that feed on the plankton. While recent studies of plankton indicate that its production is indeed down, observers don't yet have conclusive evidence on the extent of the damage to the plankton.

Researchers have known since the 1970s that chlorinated hydrocarbons (the end product of DDT and PCB) work their way into an animal's fatty tissue. High concentrations of chlorinated hydrocarbons have been found in the fat of fish and marine mammals that have died in large numbers. Though the use of DDT was banned or restricted during the 1970s, PCB continues to be used and has infiltrated the food chain.

Most recently, the mysterious deaths of dolphins off the East Coast of the United States and the deaths of seals in the Baltic Sea were a result of pinniped distemper, a disease caused by the mammals' weakened immune systems. In 1988, the Office of Naval Research and the National Marine Fisheries Service each earmarked $50,000 for a study of the deaths of dolphins along the East Coast headed by Dr. Joseph Garaci of the University of Guelph, near Toronto. Beginning in the summer of 1987, dolphins began to mysteriously wash up on the shores of New Jersey and Virginia, eventually spreading down the coast to Florida. The National Marine Fisheries Service estimates that more than 740 dolphins have died.

A study of the dolphins at Little Creek Naval Amphibious Base in Norfolk, Virginia, revealed that a type of bacteria normally noninfectious to dolphins had caused their lungs and bodies to fill with fluid as well as the appearance of lesions on their skin and mouths. Some researchers believe there may be a link between this bacteria and the dumping of toxic wastes off the New Jersey shore, though the Environmental Protection Agency says that the connection between ocean dumping and the high bacteria count cannot be confirmed.

Frustrating the study of these mysterious dolphin deaths is the lack of information scientists have on disease in living cetaceans. While the treatment of captive dolphins and porpoises tells researchers something about their susceptibility to pneumonia, parasitic diseases, and bacterial and fungal infections, conclusions about these diseases are based largely on autopsies of dead animals. Parasites such as nematodes, trematodes, hook worms, lung mites, and tape worms and other stomach worms are common. The nematodes burrow into the animal's heart, kidneys, and lungs, eventually affecting neural connections and causing tremendous pain. Many dolphins strand themselves when the pain from these parasites becomes unbearable.

Another waste in our oceans affecting dolphins and other marine mammals is long-lived plastic. From plastic bottles to the

©Robert Pitman/EarthViews

Other dangers to life at sea include major accidents, like this oil spill (left) *off the coast of San Francisco, caused by an explosion on board the ship* Puerto Rican. Above: *Two workers fight to save a stranded common dolphin's life. Even if the dolphin does make it back out to sea, a weakened dolphin has little chance of survival. In many situations, beached dolphins are sent to marine parks such as Marine World in Vallejo, California, where they are rehabilitated, and later, released. During 1987, dolphins began to wash ashore along the east coast of the United States. They suffered from weakened immune systems caused by the polluted environment.*

plastic rings that hold six-packs together, some 450,000 plastic items are dumped into the oceans every day. The real threats of plastic are its durability, transparency, and ability to float. Plastic debris, often hidden in seaweed, is eaten by dolphins and other marine mammals, puncturing or tearing their esophagi or stomachs or rupturing their intestines. Sometimes dolphins catch their fins or beaks on plastic six-pack rings and die slowly of strangulation or starvation. Plastic fishing nets, too, are difficult for dolphins and whales to detect with their sonar. When caught in them, the cetaceans may die of strangulation, drowning, or attack from other animals; sometimes they are able to swim away with part of the net wrapped around their tails, but the drag will eventually exhaust and kill them.

While the plastic industry has the resources to limit these problems—they already recycle some 20 percent of all plastic soft drink bottles—the amount of plastic that makes it into international waters far exceeds efforts to curtail this dangerous waste. Photodegradable agricultural mulch, a plastic that disintegrates in sunlight, has been available for several years but has only recently made its way into manufacture for consumer use. International laws govern the dumping of toxic chemicals and oil, but no law limits the disposal of plastics. In 1984, the Marine Entanglement Research Program was formed under the auspices of the National Oceanic and Atmospheric Administration as a result of a conference held in Honolulu.

The efforts of the National Marine Fisheries Service and other governmental agencies, coupled with the efforts of environmental groups such as Greenpeace, the Marine Mammal Fund, and the Earth Island Institute, represent the first steps in making the oceans safe for dolphins and other aquatic life. Yet, as

*T*rapped in a net, neither a pilot whale, (right),

nor a Dall's porpoise, (opposite page) has much chance for

survival.

©NMFS/Greenpeace

Ken Norris points out in *The Porpoise Watcher:* "Our myopia has led us to believe we can guide our own destiny on this planet while all other creatures must respond to the dictates of natural law." Humans must begin to realize that we are part of that "natural law." We have a tendency to think that we can "manage nature," yet whether our tampering is well-intentioned or not, we undeniably change the timbre of nature's original plan. We soon have to acknowledge that the fight for dolphins and for other wildlife survival is inextricably linked to our own.

Farley Mowat, author of numerous books about humanity's inhumanity to the earth and its living beings, hopes that we can return from our self-imposed state of alienation from nature: "Belatedly we seem to be trying to rejoin the community of living beings from which we have, for so long, alienated ourselves—and of which we have, for so long, been the mortal enemy." Many involved have suggested that respect and concern for the conservation of the earth and its inhabitants—plant, animal, and mineral—involves the maturation of a species: our own. It may be that the political action of conservation groups and the public's heightened awareness of the plight of the earth heard in the music of such groups as the Paul Winter Consort shows that we are growing out of our myopic vision to encompass a new and more enlightened one. In an interview at the Whale Center, Paul Winter said, "Whales to me are a great symbol of optimism for the possible turnaround in the downward spiral of human behavior toward Mother Earth...I see the shift in attitude toward whales and wolves and other creatures as part of that growing-up process of our culture." Perhaps we are returning to a consciousness and activism that will echo the sentiment inscribed above an ancient dolphin relief: Peace.

SELECTED BIBLIOGRAPHY

Cousteau, Jacques-Yves and Philippe Diole (translated by J.F. Bernard). *Dolphins.* New York: Arrowood Press, 1974.

Ellis, Richard. *Dolphins and Porpoises.* London: Robert Hale, 1983.

Evans, Peter G.H. *The Natural History of Whales and Dolphins.* London: Croom Helm, 1987.

Gaskin, D.E. *The Ecology of Whales and Dolphins.* London and Exeter, New Hampshire: Heinemann Educational Books Ltd., 1982.

Glueck, Nelson. *Deities and Dolphins: The Story of the Nabataeans.* New York: Farrar, Straus and Giroux, 1965.

Herman, Louis. *Cetacean Behavior.* New York: John Wiley and Sons, Publishers, 1987.

Leatherwood, Stephen and Randall R. Reeves. *The Sierra Club Handbook of Whales and Dolphins.* San Francisco: Sierra Club Books, 1983.

Lilly, John Cunningham. *Lilly on Dolphins: Humans of the Sea.* Garden City, New York: Anchor Books, 1975. (includes: *Man and Dolphin, The Mind of the Dolphin, The Dolphin in History*)

------. *Communication Between Man and Dolphin.* New York: Julian Press (member of Crown Publishing Group), 1978.

Mowat, Farley. *Sea of Slaughter.* Toronto and London: Bantam Books, 1986.

Norris, Kenneth S. *The Porpoise Watcher.* New York: W.W. Norton & Company Inc., 1974.

Norris, Kenneth S., ed. *Whales, Dolphins, and Porpoises.* Berkeley and Los Angeles: University of California Press, 1966. (collected essays of cetacean behavior, physiology, anatomy, communication, etc.)

Schusterman, Ronald, Jeanette A. Thomas, and Forrest G. Wood, eds. *Dolphin Cognition and Behavior: A Comparative Approach.* Hillsdale, New Jersey and London: Lawrence Erlbaum Associates, Publishers, 1986.

Steiner, Todd, David Phillis and Mark J. Palmer. *The Tragedy Continues: Killing of Dolphins by the Tuna Industry.* San Francisco, California: Earth Island Institute and Oakland, California: Whale Center, Spring, 1988.

Stonehouse, Bernard. *Sea Mammals of the World.* Harmondsworth: Penguin Books, 1985.

Wood, Forrest G. *Marine Mammals and Man: The Navy's Porpoises and Sea Lions.* Washington and New York: Robert B. Luce Inc., 1973.

SOURCES

Environmental and Conservation Groups

Earth Island Institute
300 Broadway, Suite 28
San Francisco, CA 94133

Environmental Defense Fund
257 Park Avenue South
New York, NY 10010

Environmental Policy Institute
218 D Street, SE
Washington, DC 20003

Friends of the Earth
377 City Road
London, EC1

Greenpeace
30 Islington Green
London, N1

Marine Mammal Fund
Fort Mason Center
Building E
San Francisco, CA 94123

National Wildlife Federation
1326 Massachusetts Avenue, NW
mail to: 1412 16th Street
Washington, DC 20036

Oceanic Society
Suite E-225
Fort Mason Center
San Francisco, CA 94123

The Pink Dolphin Project
P.O. Box 38037
Hollywood, CA 90038

Sierra Club (Headquarters)
730 Polk Street
San Francisco, CA 94109
  or 330 Pennsylvania Avenue, SE
  Washington, DC 20003

Whale Center
3929 Piedmont Avenue
Oakland, CA 94611

WorldWildlife Fund UK
Panda House
Weyside Park
Godalming
Surrey, GU7 1XR

Government Agencies

Environmental Protection
 Agency
Enforcement and Compliance
 Monitoring
401 M Street, SW
Washington, DC 20460

House Merchant Marine
 and Fisheries Committee
Subcommittee on Fisheries and
 Wildlife Conservation and the
 Environment
543 HOB Annex #2
Washington, DC 20515

Ministry of Agriculture, Fisheries
 and Food
Whitehall Place
London, SW1

National Oceanic and
 Atmospheric Administration
 (Commerce Department)
14th Street & Constitution
 Avenue, NW
Washington, DC 20230

Marine and Estuarine
 Management
1825 Connecticut Avenue, NW
Washington, DC 20235

National Environmental Satellite,
 Data, and Information Service
Federal Building 4
Suitland, MD 20233

National Marine Fisheries
 Service
1825 Connecticut Avenue, NW
Washington, DC 20235

Ocean Assessments
11400 Rockville Pike
Rockville, MD 20852

Senate Environment and Public
 Works Committee
Subcommittee on Environmental
 Protection
SH-408
Washington, DC 20510

Research Centers

California Academy of Sciences
Golden Gate Park
San Francisco, CA 94118

Institute of Marine Studies
University of College of Swansea
Singleton Park
Swansea
West Glamorgan, SA2 8PP

Institute of Oceanographic Studies
Brook Road
Wormley
Godalming
Surrey, GU8 5UB

Narragansett Marine Laboratory
University of Rhode Island
Kingston, RI

National Marine Mammal
  Laboratory
7600 Sand Point Way, NE
Building 4
Seattle, WA 98115

Natural History Museum of
  Los Angeles County
900 Exposition Boulevard
Los Angeles, CA 90007

Sea Mammal Research Unit
c/o British Antarctic Survey
Madingley Road
Cambridge, CB3 0ET

Smithsonian Environmental
  Research Center
(Smithsonian Institution)
P.O. Box 28
Contees Wharf Road
Edgewater, MD 21037

University of California at
  Santa Cruz
Marine Sciences Division
Long Marine Laboratory
  and Friends of Long Marine
Laboratory
c/o Institute of Marine Sciences
Santa Cruz, CA 95064

Woods Hole Oceanographic
  Institution
Woods Hole, MA 02543

Marine Parks and Aquariums

Brighton Aquarium
Marine Parade
Brighton
Sussex, BN2 1TB

Busch Gardens—The Dark
  Continent
3000 Busch Boulevard
Tampa, FL 33601

Disneyland
1313 Harbor Boulevard
Anaheim, CA 92802

Disney World/Epcot Center
P.O. Box 10,000
Lake Buena Vista, FL 32830

Marine World/Africa USA
Marine World Parkway
Vallejo, CA 94589

Marineland of Florida
9507 Ocean Shore Blvd.
Marineland, FL 32086

Miami Seaquarium
4400 Rickenbacker Causeway
Miami, FL 33149

New England Aquarium
Central Wharf
Boston, MA 02110

New York Aquarium
Surf Avenue and West 8th Street
Coney Island
Brooklyn, NY

Ocean World
1701 SE 17th Street
Fort Lauderdale, FL 33316

Sea-Arama Marineworld
P.O. Box 3068
Galveston, TX 77552

Sea Life Park
Makapuu Point
Waimanalo, HI 96795

Sea World
1720 South Shores Road
San Diego, CA 92109

Sea World of Chicago
4640 North Clark Street
Chicago, IL 60640

Sea World of Florida
7007 Sea World Drive
Orlando, FL 32821

Sea World of Ohio
1100 Sea World Drive
Aurora, OH 44202

Sea World of Texas
10500 Sea World Drive
San Antonio, TX 78251

Windsor Safari Park
Winkfield Road
Windsor
Berks, SL4 4AY

The Zoological Society of London
Whipsnade Park
near Dunstable, LU6 2LF

INDEX

A

Aesop's Fables, 18
Altruism, 92, 105
Amazon River, threat to
    dolphins in, 129
Anatomy and physiology
    brain, 97–98
    circulatory system, 46–48
    digestive system, 46–48
    fins and flippers, 53
    locomotion and, 44–45
    respiratory system, 42
    stomach, 48
    thermoregulation, 42
Archaeocetes
    evolution and taxonomy of, 32
    extinction of, 35
Aristotle, 18

Atlantic white-sided dolphins.
    See Lagenorhynchus sp.

B

*Balaena assasina. See Orcinus
    orca*
Baleen whales, 25
Beiji. *See Lipotes vexillifer*
Blood makeup and circulation,
    42
Blood typing, 82
Blubber, 42, 45
Body temperature, 42
Bottlenose dolphin. *See
    Tursiops* sp.
Boutu. *See Inia geoffrensis*
Brain, 97–98
Bulgaria, dolphin hunting
    ended by, 129
Burmeister's porpoise. *See
    Phocoena spinipinnis*

C

Campbell, Joseph, 21, 96
Captivity
    behavioral changes in, 113–14
    capture and transport, 111–14
    for entertainment, 109
    intelligence and, 100
Carson, Rachel, 132
Cephalorynchus sp., 55, 57, 68

Cetaceans
    bone structure, 24
    dolphins and porpoises
        compared, 39–40, 51–53
    endangered species, 121–23,
        129
    evolution. *See* Evolution
    pollution and, 132–36
    taxonomic schema, 25, 32,
        55, 69
    See also specific cetaceans;
        Dolphins; Porpoises
Chile, dolphin hunting legal in,
    130
Circulatory system, 42
Clacton Pier Seaquarium
    (England), 130
CMS News, 84
Cochito. *See Phocoena Sinus*
Commerson's dolphin. *See
    Cephalorynchus* sp.
Common dolphin. *See
    Delphinus delphis*
Communication, 84
    anthropomorphic view of, 96
    intelligence and, 100–105
Condylarthra, 32
Council of Europe, Convention
    on the Conservation of
    European Wildlife and
    Natural Habitats, 129–30
Cousteau, Jacques, 109
Crete (ancient), 14
Cytogenetics, 29